OXFORD
INDIA SHORT
INTRODUCTIONS

CASTE

The Oxford India Short
Introductions are concise,
stimulating, and accessible guides
to different aspects of India.
Combining authoritative analysis,
new ideas, and diverse perspectives,
they discuss subjects which are
topical yet enduring, as also
emerging areas of study and debate.

OXFORD
INDIA SHORT
INTRODUCTIONS
CASTE

SURINDER S. JODHKA

OXFORD
UNIVERSITY PRESS

OXFORD
UNIVERSITY PRESS

Oxford University Press is a department of the University of Oxford.
It furthers the University's objective of excellence in research, scholarship,
and education by publishing worldwide. Oxford is a registered trademark of
Oxford University Press in the UK and in certain other countries

Published in India by
Oxford University Press
YMCA Library Building, 1 Jai Singh Road, New Delhi 110 001, India

© Oxford University Press 2012

The moral rights of the author have been asserted

First Edition published in 2012
Second impression 2013

ISBN-13: 978-0-19-808936-0
ISBN-10: 0-19-808936-8

Typeset in 11/15.6 Bembo Std
by Excellent Laser Typesetters, Pitampura, Delhi 110 034
Printed in India at G.H. Prints Pvt. Ltd, New Delhi 110 020

To the memory of Krishna Raj, the former editor of the
Economic and Political Weekly,
who until the last day of his life, worked tirelessly to
facilitate serious academic discussions on
issues of contemporary concern

Contents

Tables

Preface

Why should we talk about caste? Does caste really matter today beyond one's family and personal life? If yes, for whom does it matter and in what ways? How should we talk about caste in the twenty-first century? What has changed and what remains of it in contemporary India? What are the operational parameters of caste in present-day urban society and its economy? How do we understand its association with democratic politics and/or its politicization? Do caste-based quotas and reservations strengthen divisions in society? How does the reality of caste play out in modern-day labour markets, in the informal sector and the corporate economy?

These may appear to be simple and straightforward questions. However, given the diversity of perspectives and patterns of change being experienced in Indian society, it is not very easy to provide simple answers to these questions. This short introduction tries to engage with the contemporary reality of caste with all these questions in the background and attempts to provide a critical introduction to different perspectives on the subject.

We could approach the caste question from a wide variety of perspectives—custom, ritual, tradition, or even religion. This 'short' introduction interrogates caste primarily from the perspective of inequality.

Inequality is an endemic feature of human societies. Notwithstanding the growing acceptance of the ideal of equality, citizenship, and democratic forms of governance across cultures and countries of the world, inequalities—old and new—have continued to persist and grow. Older forms of inequality, of race, caste, gender, or ethnicity, have indeed changed with time but they have certainly not disappeared. This is despite the concerted efforts of a variety of actors against such practices. The contemporary world has also seen a manifold increase in newer forms of inequalities— of income, occupational prestige, and its many other manifestations. We live with paradoxes. Caste is one such paradox.

Sociologists have often described caste as a 'closed system' of stratification where social groups, often divided on the basis of their occupation, strictly follow the code of behaviour prescribed by tradition regarding marriage and kinship alliances. Caste groups are unequal, ranked on a scale of hierarchy based on their ritual status, from pure to impure. Their 'status' or position in the system determines with whom they can interact and with whom they cannot. The idea and practice of untouchability is an integral part of the caste system.

Like any other institution or practice, caste has been changing over time. How do we make sense of the caste question today?

Ever since its early conceptualizations, the subject of caste has not been a monopoly of sociologists or other social scientists alone. A wide variety of actors, for a wide variety of reasons, have written about or taken interest in caste, social science academics being just one of them. More interestingly, perhaps, hardly ever has academic research alone shaped the discourse on caste, as indeed on many other social processes that are of critical contemporary significance. From classical orientalist writings to the contemporary writings on Dalit political agency, social science scholarship on caste has invariably been embedded in politics of one kind or the other. This is not to suggest that the contemporary scholarship on caste has only followed the 'politics of caste' but to underline the point that it is hard to pursue a purely academic research on a subject like caste.

The question of caste today is also complicated by the fact that it has remained deeply embedded in the questions of 'Indian modernity'. This is evident from the ensemble of words through which the category of caste is invoked—'tradition', 'nativity', 'custom', 'ritual', 'backwardness', or 'exclusion'—all of which generate strong political effects. The words that are often invoked in opposition to caste, such as 'development', 'progress', 'merit', or 'inclusion' and 'citizenship' also generate equally strong political effects. This complicated nature of the relationship of caste with modernity has continued to be a source of contention in the writings and discussions on the subject even today.

Caste has also been an important axis around which the West has engaged with India. Hierarchies of divisions have existed in the subcontinent in a wide variety of ways for a very long time. However, these were first articulated in the language of caste, as we understand it today, by travellers from the West. Even the word 'caste' has its origin in the writings of Portuguese seafarers who arrived on the west coast of India for trade. The later orientalists and British colonial administrators developed 'theories' of the caste system, which helped them make sense of India and situate it in their emerging perspectives on human evolution. These writings turned out to be extremely influential in shaping the later sociological and social anthropological conceptualizations of caste. These theories about the caste system and Indian society also played a critical role in shaping the nationalist imaginations of Indian tradition, and over the years, became a constitutive element of the Indian self.

Since the 1950s, the process of economic growth and institutionalization of democratic politics have transformed almost every aspect of Indian society, including the institution of caste. However, the reality of caste has certainly not disappeared. Though in some cases caste groups have horizontally consolidated themselves into 'caste associations' and political formations, the elements of hierarchy and inequality continue to be reproduced even today in many different ways. In other words, caste is alive and kicking, not merely in the form of substantialized identities but also as a source of privileges and deprivations. Instead of it fading away, many would argue that the public presence of caste has grown in India over the years.

Caste has also remained a very active and interesting area of research. Apart from sociologists and social anthropologists, historians, political scientists, economists, and even creative writers have written a great deal on different dimensions of the subject. They have also been working with a wide variety of conceptual frameworks and political sensibilities. Over the years, caste has become an important factor in the democratic political process. The state policy of quotas and political mobilization of communities have changed the *value* of caste in contemporary India. Caste today is an important element of public policy, not only for the developmental state but also for the global funding agencies and civil society groups engaged with questions of poverty and exclusion.

This 'short' introduction explores and introduces this diverse and divergent terrain of caste in contemporary India. Though it does so by looking at the available literature on caste, the book is not simply a review of the existing literature or an analysis of the trends of research on the subject. What it tries is to make sense of the changing perspectives and meanings of caste in the social science writings, and in the popular discourse on the subject, over the last century and more. I have tried to present the discussion in a simple and accessible language but without being simplistic. Attempting to reconcile the multiple and conflicting viewpoints on a subject like caste that emanate from varied political locations and subject positions will perhaps not be a very prudent exercise.

Acknowledgements

For a sociologist working in/on India it is almost imperative to have some understanding of the basic literature on the subject of caste. This invariably extends to also having a political position on 'what is happening to caste' and 'how the Indian state should deal with it'. However, notwithstanding this predicament, I strongly feel that there is a space for objective engagements with the subject and its social and political dynamics in contemporary India, through empirical documentations of the diverse patterns of change on the ground and scholarly deliberations on its various manifestations and metamorphoses.

This short introduction has emerged out of my own engagements with the subject of caste. Apart from the empirical studies I have carried out over the past decade and more, I have also learnt a great deal from my discussions and interactions with fellow scholars. I would like to particularly acknowledge Ghanshyam Shah, André Béteille, Dipankar Gupta, Gurpreet Mahajan, Gurharpal Singh, D.N. Dhanagare, and P.N. Pimpley. I have also gained a lot from my interactions with Sukhadeo Thorat, Sudha Pai, Gopal Guru, James Manor, Satish Deshpande, and John Harriss. My engagement with the Dalit question provided me a different perspective. I am particularly grateful to Maitreyi Das, Maritn Macwan, Ramya Subrahmanian, Anand Bolimera, Sobin George, and Paul Diwakar who made me think about caste in relation to developmental and social policy. Discussions with my colleagues at the Centre for the Study of Social Systems, particularly Vivek Kumar and G. Srinivas, have been fruitful.

The support I receive from Sneha, my wife, in my academic work is always very valuable. Apart from reading and commenting on my chapters, she helps me refine my ideas and arguments. Writer and long-time friend Jaspreet Singh also read the draft and gave insightful comments. Two of my students, Anasua Chatterjee and Ujithra Ponniah, helped me complete this work on time. I am grateful to them.

1

Caste as Tradition

[While supervising the Census work in the late nineteenth century]...the Census Commissioner for India
complained from Bengal that 'the ignorant classes have
very little idea of what caste means and are prone to
return either their occupation, or their sub-caste, or
their clan, or else some title by which they are known
to their fellow villagers'...but in the twentieth century, with census after census and more and more
inquiries from strangers requiring people to identify
caste, many became schooled in the proper answer.
(Charsley 1996: 3)

The term 'caste', used to describe a system of social
relations that is considered to be uniquely Indian, and
that presumably distinguishes the traditional Indian
society from the West, is ironically not of Indian origin.

As is well known, the term comes from the Spanish word *casta*, meaning race. The Portuguese seafarers, who arrived on the west coast of India for trade in the fifteenth century, were the first ones to use it in the Indian context. In the popular understanding, caste is an ancient institution of the Hindus, based on the ideas of *varna, karma,* and *dharma* pronounced in a text called the *Manusmriti*. These ideas translated into a hierarchical society, structured around the notions of purity and pollution. The varna system divided the Hindus into four mutually exclusive categories—the Brahmins, the Kshatriyas, the Vaishyas, and the Shudras. Beyond the four varnas were the *achhoot*s (the untouchables). These four or five categories occupied different positions in the status hierarchy, with the Brahmins at the top, followed by the other three varnas in the order mentioned above, with the achhoots occupying a position at the very bottom.

Caste, according to this 'textbook' view, was a pan-Indian social system with little or no variations across regions. It also remained virtually unchanged over centuries, from the times of its origin in the ancient past up to the British colonial rule, when the colonial state introduced a fundamentally different social and

economic regime. With the process of Westernization/
modernization, unleashed during the colonial period
and accelerated by the Indian state after its independence in 1947, the spread of 'secular' education and
the growing influence of urban culture caused caste
to gradually decline. Caste, it is argued, would have
nearly disappeared by now had the wily politicians
not mobilized the 'primordial sentiments' of the
common people for their narrow political and electoral gains.

However, an opposite view is equally popular.
Many, drawing their understanding of caste from similar sources, would argue the fact that caste continues
to survive in some form or the other in present-day
India is enough to establish that nothing worthwhile
has changed in the underlying ideological structure of
the Hindu mind. India's modernization or the associated processes of development, democratic governance
and secularization are all superficial. The essential
realities of caste, inequality and social exclusion,
largely survive.

These indeed are oversimplified views of a complex reality. The lived experience of caste and a large
volume of social science research contradict such

3

formulations of the caste system and the patterns of social change in contemporary India. The problem begins with the underlying assumptions of the classical formulation. First, while ideology is indeed an important element of caste, its life extends beyond religious belief. The materiality of caste is as important, if not more, as its ideology, and it is hard to reduce it to a mere consequential effect of a religious practice.

It is common knowledge that caste-like divisions have existed and continue to exist among followers of other faith systems, Muslims, Christians, Sikhs, and even Buddhists, living in the subcontinent, and beyond. The structures of caste have close ties with other social, economic, and political systems, such as kinship, power regimes, and labour relations. As would be the case with any other social institution and ideological system, relations of caste would have also changed with transformations in the larger social and economic structures. Second, notwithstanding some common features across the subcontinent, the nature and practice of caste relations varied significantly across regions of the subcontinent. The regional histories and other processes of change in social life have shaped the ground realities of caste. Third, caste has also always been a contested institution. Various religious and 'secular' movements have questioned the ideological groundings of caste, well before Western modernity arrived in the subcontinent. However, despite these obvious and well-known facts, the popular notion of caste has prevailed.

Why has this happened? How did this view of caste develop? What makes a particular theory so influential that it becomes a commonsense view of caste? We begin this chapter by looking at the early conceptu-alizations or theories of Indian society and their influ-ence on the thinking of Indian nationalists, which in turn influenced the framing of 'the idea of India', as we understand it today. An important element of the 'idea of India' is the notion of an 'Indian tradition'. Though several elements have indeed come from the past, the Indian tradition is essentially a modern construct. A particular view of caste and Hinduism is central to this notion of Indian tradition and much of it has been constructed out of the Indological writings on Indian civilization, colonial administrative reports and the nationalist imaginations (including the social and religious reform movements) during the nine-teenth and early twentieth centuries.

Caste as the 'Indian Tradition'

Varna, jati, or *zat* and many other similar terms have been in use in different parts of the South Asian region for a very long time. They describe a variety of prevailing social divisions and hierarchies of status and class. This indeed includes the idea and practice of pollution or untouchability. However, the history of modern-day theorization of caste begins with Western and colonial encounters with the Indian civilization.

The term caste, as mentioned earlier, was the English translation of the Spanish word *casta,* first used in the Indian context by the Portuguese seafarers. Other Europeans, attracted by India for various reasons, followed the Portuguese. The British proved to be the most important of them. Not only were they successful colonizers, but they also wrote a great deal on the social and cultural life of the Indian people. For the colonial rulers, such theorization of the Indian social order was not merely an academic exercise. This helped them make sense of what seemed like an incomprehensible reality. They also deployed their notion of caste hierarchy in their administrative system for classifying the native communities and determining their qualities and traits. As Sharma points out:

> … the British took the existence of caste very seriously. Successive censuses of India attempted to classify the entire population by caste, on the assumption that everyone must belong to some caste or other and that castes were real identifiable groups. As a result, this objectification of caste actually made it more real and liable to rigidification … (2002: 8)

The Western view of caste developed over time, with the writings of orientalists, missionaries, and colonial administrators contributing in different ways.

The orientalists believed that the best way to make sense of Indian society was by reading the classical texts of Hinduism. They learnt Sanskrit and collaborated with 'pundits and *sastri*s' to access and understand the textual sources. The orientalists presented a rather simplistic view of the caste system. They theorized caste as a hierarchical system through the idea of varna as a substantive category where the Brahmins were always placed at the top of the hierarchical order, followed by Kshatriya, Vaishya, and Shudra. The untouchable communities were outside the formal hierarchy but their status also followed this neat hierarchical ordering derived from the logic of purity and impurity.

However, such a textual understanding of India had many inherent biases. As Cohn rightly argues,

> The acceptance of a textural view of the society ... also led to a picture of Indian society as being static, time-less and space-less. Statements about customs which derived from third century A.D. texts and observations from the late eighteenth century were equally good evidence for determining the nature of society and culture in India. In this view of Indian society there was no regional variation and no questioning of the relationship between prescriptive normative state-ments derived from the texts and the actual behavior of individuals and groups. Indian society was seen as a set of rules which every Hindu followed. (1968: 7–8)

The ground realities of the Indian society, however, did not easily concur with the varna model of caste. The colonial administrators had to revise their under-standing of the systems of hierarchy. As they extended their rule and explored different regions of India, they were confronted with diversities. This became most evident when they started classifying Indians on the lines of caste for enumerating the Indian population for the Census. The varna system was only useful to the extent of being a model, a framework of hierarchy. The ground reality of caste was much too diverse and complex to fit into a simple model. The idea of varna had to be distinguished from the jati, the actual social units, or the concrete endogamous social group-ings. Unlike the varna system, which was presumably a pan-Indian system, the jatis had a regional charac-ter. Every region had a large number of jatis and its subunits, ranging between 200 to 300 or even more. Their names and associated social correlates also varied across regions. However, while they recognized these empirical diversities, the colonial administrators con-tinued to treat caste as a unified system of hierarchy with common features across the subcontinent. It will be worthwhile to quote Cohn once again on this: 'India was seen as a collection of castes; the particular picture was different in any given time and place, but India was a sum of its parts and the parts were castes' (Cohn 1968: 16).

Similarly, Nicholas Dirks argues that caste was widely recognized by the colonial regime 'as a local form of "civil society", which was responsible for India's "political weakness" and symptom of the over-development of its religious preoccupations' (Dirks 2001:40). He claims that by 1885 there was: '... general recognition that caste was the foundational fact of Indian society, fundamental both to Hinduism (as Hinduism was to it) and to the Indian subcontinent as a civilizational region' (Ibid.: 41).

This colonial view of caste has also been extremely influential among a section of Western scholars who have attempted to theorize caste as a specific system of social relations. Some of them have extensively used the orientalist writings on India and administrative reports of the colonial officials while trying to provide descriptive accounts and theories of the caste system. There is also an overlap of the colonial administrative view of caste and the scholarship on Indian society. For example, after completing his administrative career in India, J.H. Hutton took up professorship at the Cambridge University and wrote a book *Caste in India* (1946).

One of the major concerns of the orientalist and colonial administrators was to identify the origin of the system of caste in India. They speculated on the possible explanations of the caste system in Hinduism, as originating from the racial mix-up after the Aryans arrived in the ancient past or simply in the evolutionary process and division of labour. Some Indian scholars also wrote in a similar vein. G.S. Ghurye, for example, identified six core features of the Hindu caste system:

Segmental division of society: Castes were groups with well-developed lifestyles of their own. The membership of the groups was determined by birth and not by choice. The status of a person depended not on the amount of wealth he possessed but on the rank that his caste enjoyed in the Hindu society.

Hierarchy: There was a definite scheme of social precedence amongst castes. Each group occupied a specific status in the overall framework of hierarchy.

Restrictions on social intercourse: The Hindu society had minute rules about social relations. It, for example, imposed restrictions on what sort of food or drink the members of one caste could accept from the members of another caste.

Civil and religious disabilities and privileges: Segregation of individual castes or groups of castes in the village was the most obvious mark of civil privileges and disabilities. Certain sacraments could not be performed by any caste other than the Brahmins. Similarly, Shudras and other lower castes were not allowed to read or learn the sacred scriptures.

Restricted choice of occupation: Generally, each caste considered a particular occupation as its legitimate calling. To abandon the hereditary occupation in pursuit of another, even when it was more lucrative, was not considered right.

Restrictions on marriage: Caste groups observed strict endogamy. Members of a caste group married only within their castes. However, there were a few exceptions. In some regions of India, the upper-caste man could marry a lower-caste woman, an alliance known in kinship studies as hypergamy.

The subject of caste also figures in the Western classical sociological writings. The well-known German sociologist, Max Weber, for example, viewed the Indian caste system as an extreme of, what he described as 'status groups', which were present in all societies where market or capitalist relations had not yet evolved. Status groups were like ethnic communities, completely closed to outsiders, and sharing some form of 'social estimation of honour'. Birth within the group, like an ethnic group, determined the membership of a caste group. However, unlike other ethnic communities, castes were also hierarchical and the order of hierarchy was acceptable to those lower down in the hierarchy. While Weber accepted the 'orientalist' view about the rigidity and unchanging nature of caste, he did not think that the presence of caste-like status groups was peculiar to India or Hindus (Gerth and Mills 1948: 189; Sharma 2002: 12), though caste may be an extreme form of the system of status hierarchies.

However, it is in the writings of a French scholar, Célestin Bouglé, that we can see the beginning of a systematic theory of the caste system, which derives the substance of its arguments from the colonial and orientalist writings. For Bouglé, caste was indeed a system of inequality and though in its purest form it developed among the Hindus, it was not peculiar to India. It is '...no more than the synthesis of elements which are present everywhere' (Bouglé 1958: 30). He identified three core elements that make caste: hereditary specialization, hierarchy, and repulsion. In caste society, 'the son of a blacksmith will be a black-smith just as the son of a warrior will be a warrior'. Further,

> The word caste makes us think not only of heredi-tarily appointed work but also of unequally divided rights. To say caste is not to say monopoly only but also privilege. By the fact of his birth one indi-vidual is bound to pay heavy taxes while another escapes them. In the eyes of justice this man is 'worth' a hundred pieces of gold and that one is only fifty. (Ibid.: 8–9)

Perhaps the most important and critical feature of caste is the third one:

> When we say ... the spirit of caste ... we mean that the different groups ... repel each other rather than attract, that each retires within itself, isolates itself, makes every effort to prevent its members from con-tracting alliance or even from entering relations with neighbouring groups ... [I]t is ... designed to atom-ize the societies into which it penetrates; it divides them ... into a multitude of opposed fragments; it brings each of their element groups face to face, sepa-rated by a mutual repulsion. (Ibid.: 9)

Thus, the definition of a caste-based society, argued Bouglé, is that 'it is divided into a large number of mutually opposed groups which are hereditarily specialized and hierarchically arranged'. For Célestin Bouglé, as for Max Weber, though in its 'pure' form caste was found in India, it was not peculiarly an Indian institution. However, both also underlined the point that caste was not simply a manifestation of class difference. Its core elements were derived from the given cultural tradition (honour and repulsion) and specific institutional arrangements (hereditary occupations and hierarchy).

Louis Dumont and the Book-view of Caste

Some time later, another French scholar, Louis Dumont, extended Bouglé's theory to an extreme view, which looked at caste as a peculiarly Hindu practice and he contrasted the Indian culture with the Western society. While the West was a modern society based on the ideas of individualism and equality, India was a traditional culture. The social structures of a traditional society like India functioned on very different principles and ought to be studied through the perspectives or methods of 'totality' and 'holism'. The traditional caste society valued 'totality' while the modern societies of the West valued 'individual'. Unlike the modern societies of the West, the ideas of 'equality' among individuals were not the structural features of Indian culture. The Hindu mind was concerned with maintaining social difference and inequalities (as in *Homo Hierarchichus*).

Following the orientalists, Dumont too referred to the classical Hindu scriptures for understanding the underlying ideological structure of the caste system. The core element in the ideology of caste, for Dumont, was hierarchy. 'The castes,' Dumont argued, 'teach us a fundamental social principle, hierarchy.' Underlining the ancient and religious nature of caste, he argued that some eight centuries before Christ the Hindus established an absolute distinction between power and hierarchical status. Hierarchy was the essence of caste. The idea of inequality in the caste system was not simply an opposite idea of 'equality', as the modern West understands the term. Caste system represents a particular type of inequality, that is, hierarchy, naturalized inequality, inherently legitimized by the Hindu religious belief.

The caste system, therefore 'was above all a system of ideas and values' and it ought not to be treated as an extension of the political and economic relations, the material world. In other words, ideology for him was not a residual category, a part of superstructure, as the Marxist theory elaborates it. In his framework, ideology is an autonomous sphere and could not be reduced to any other factor or treated secondary to politico-economic factors.

Though Dumont acknowledged Bouglé's contributions to the theorization of caste and his ability to identify the three core features of the system, he found it wanting. For a proper theoretical explanation of the system, he argued, we should be able to identify one common element, 'a single true principle' to which the three features of the caste system suggested by Bouglé could be reduced. Such a principle, Dumont suggested, was 'the opposition of the pure and the impure'. Hierarchy, defined as superiority of the pure over the impure, was the keystone in Dumont's model of the caste system. As Dumont writes:

> This opposition underlies hierarchy, which is the
> superiority of the pure to the impure, underlies

separation because the pure and the impure must be kept separate, and underlies the division of labour because pure and impure occupations must likewise be kept separate. The whole is founded on the necessary and hierarchical coexistence of the two opposites. (1998: 43)

The opposition of pure and impure, for Dumont was the underlying structural logic of the ideology of caste, which translated into a society based on the principle of hierarchy. Following this, he would argue that the two extremes of the system of caste hierarchy are the Brahmin at one end and the untouchable at the other. The pure must 'find its logical opposite, the impure, for it to be a complete system' (Gupta 1981: 2095; also see Quigley 1993: 27–9).

As mentioned earlier, unlike Weber and Bouglé, Dumont believed in the peculiar nature of Indian society and contrasted the foundational values of Indian society with those of the West. He did so by pointing to the differing nature of the relationship between 'status' and 'power' in the two societies. Power and status normally went together in modern societies of the West. In India, however, there was a divergence between the two. In a caste-based social system, those who were the most powerful politically and economically did not necessarily enjoy the highest status in society. Likewise, those who enjoyed the highest status (the Brahmins) could be economically poor and with no political power. In other words, according to Dumont, the priest in India (the Brahmin) occupied a superior position vis-à-vis the king (or the dominant caste) because in the Hindu caste society, status as a principle of social organization was superior to the principle of power. *Status encompassed power.* This was only an extension of the ideology of the dialectical opposition and hierarchical relationship of pure and impure in the Hindu caste system.

Assessing Dumont

Dumont's book on the Indian caste system has perhaps been the single most influential academic work on the subject. However, his theory has also been one of the most criticized academic writings on caste, and for good reasons. It will be useful to critically examine Dumont's propositions because they represent the classical Western thinking on the subject of caste and on the Indian society in general.

Dumont's book, particularly after its English edition became available, has been widely discussed by the students of Indian society all over the world. Though it continues to be an important text on the subject, its criticisms have also been very extensive and wide ranging.

Many students of Indian society have accused him of an ideological bias, for presenting a one-sided view of caste. His theory, critiques argue, provides an account of the caste system that the Brahmins would have liked to tell, a Brahmanical view of caste. Given that his sources were mostly textual, which the Brahmins would have written and retained, his view of caste was indeed one-sided. Scholars have pointed out that he ignored the large amount of empirical literature that was available to him, produced by professional social anthropologists in the form of village studies and monographs which provided graphic details of the ways in which the caste system functioned at the micro-level simply because they did not conform to his notion of caste. Even his choice of textual sources was selective. The classical Indian textual sources do not provide such a unified and singular view of caste (Das and Uberoi 1971). Historians point out that even in the ancient times, caste was a contested and evolving reality and like other aspects of Indian society, it continued to change with time. For example, the status of Brahmins in a given region or kingdom depended on their relationship with the king. Only when Brahmins became priests of the king or acquired control over large amounts of land did they begin to enjoy high status (see Thapar 1975; Gupta 1981).

Dumont would argue in his defence that he had only tried to build a theory that provided an understanding of the underlying structure of the caste system and not the way people practised it in their everyday life. The pure hierarchy is a 'state of mind'. However, the critics argue, the 'state of mind' becomes sociologically important only when it translates into action and social relations. As Berreman points out, caste did not exist except empirically, in the lives of people as they interacted with each other. The fact is that the lived experience of caste was very different from what Dumont seemed to suggest. 'The human meaning of caste for those who lived it was power and vulnerability, privilege and oppression, honour and denigration, plenty and want, reward and deprivation, security and anxiety' (Berreman 1991: 87–8).

21

Similarly, Joan Mencher who conducted her field-work among the lower castes in a south India village reported that from the point of view of people at the lowest end of the scale, caste had functioned and continued to function as a very effective system of economic exploitation (Mencher 1974). Fuller also made a related point in his writings criticizing Dumont's theory. He argues that it is not only the relations of power that his theory undervalues; such a notion of caste also undermines the obvious facts about the inequalities in material life and the role caste played in their reproduction. In his study of the redistributive system prevailing in pre-colonial India, Fuller showed how village level system of caste relations was integrated into a larger political authority, beyond the village (Fuller 1977; 1984). James Manor too argues that 'The old caste hierarchies were rooted in materiality. They did not just exist in people's minds—at the level of ideas, beliefs and imaginings ... Caste and caste hierarchies had—and still have—tangible substance' (Manor 2010: xxii).

Another Indian sociologist, André Béteille (1986) criticized Dumont for overemphasizing the difference between India and the West, the former being a society characterized by holism and hierarchy and the latter by individualism and equality. A comparative account of the West and India, if it was to be based on empirical researches on the two settings, would not be as contrasting as presented by Dumont. In the process he also ends up presenting a homogenous view of Indian society where 'hierarchy and the sole value of purity encompass all aspects of inter-caste relationships', which in turn 'entail a rejection of all other possible indigenous meanings and values in these relationships' (Raheja 1989: 81).

Why has Dumont's theory of caste then been so popular? Arjun Appadurai offers an interesting answer to this question. The concept of 'hierarchy' provides a useful 'shorthand for summarizing the cultural complexities' and diversities that a historical and ethnographic account of the past traditions of the land would provide. Secondly, it obviously captures something important. Even though one may question its exact status, the idea of 'hierarchy is undeniably a striking feature of Indian society'. It has come to represent the distinctiveness of the Indian society (Appadurai 1988: 44–5). In the process, Appadurai contends with Béteille and many others that such a theory of India also

23

reinforces the classical orientalist view of India, which essentializes India as a land of religion (Hinduism). It also presents India to the West as a 'different', the other of the West, an exotic land, with strange practices. It *totalizes* India by 'making specific features of a society's thought or practice not only its essence but also its totality' (Ibid.: 41). In other words, everything else that is part of the Indian social and cultural life is either reducible to caste or is of no significance. This 'othering' of India in the 'book-view' of caste presented Indian society as having a social order that had been static for ages with no possibility of change emanating from internal contradictions. The natives had no agency of their own to be able to change (Inden 1990: 65); the argument thus working as an ideological justification for India's colonization by the West.

The 'Field-view' of Caste: Village Society and Indian Tradition

As a counterpoint to the 'book-view' of Indian society, social scientists, particularly social anthropologists, as they began to work on the Indian society during the middle of the twentieth century, recognized the need for constructing a fieldwork-based or 'field-view' of the traditional Indian social order. Such an understanding was required not only for correcting the classical Hindu religious text-based understanding (book-view) of India but also for working out policies for social change and development that were to be introduced by the Indian state after its independence from colonial rule.

Given that nearly 85 per cent of all Indians lived in its more than 5 million villages, the 'field-view' of India was to be constructed through the study of village society. As the colonial administrators had repeatedly stressed in their writings, the distinctive feature of the traditional Indian village life was its order of caste hierarchy. Caste relations presumably worked in their classical form in the village setting. Caste and village were, therefore, often used as hyphenated categories in the available literature on Indian society.

Using the classical method of long-drawn ethnographic fieldwork, individual social anthropologists carried out a large number of 'village studies' by living in a single village. After living with the community for a period of one to two years, the anthropologist provided a descriptive account of the different aspects of the social and cultural life of the village. A village, for them, was not simply a settlement. It also had a methodological value, an entry point into the traditional social life of India. As one of them wrote, a village represented 'India in microcosm' (Hoebel in Hiebert 1971: vii). Another scholar described villages as 'invaluable observation-centres' where an anthropologist could 'study in detail social processes and problems to be found occurring in great parts of India, if not in a great part of the world' (Srinivas 1955: 99). Villages were supposed to have been around for 'hundreds of years', having 'survived years of wars, making and breaking up of empires, famines, floods and other natural disasters'. They were the 'principal social and administrative unit'. This perceived 'historical continuity and stability of villages' strengthened the case for village studies' (Dasgupta 1978: 1).

Based on such field studies, social anthropologists published a large number of monographs during the 1950s and 1960s. Several of these studies reported that the 'village communities' all over the Indian subcontinent had a number of common features. 'Different castes and communities inhabiting the village were integrated in its economic, social, and ritual pattern by ties of mutual and reciprocal obligations sanctioned and sustained by generally accepted conventions' (Dube 1960: 202). Wiser, in *The Hindu Jajmani System,* first published in 1936, conceptualized the social relationships among caste groups in the Indian village in the framework of 'reciprocity'. The framework of reciprocity implied that though the village as a social organization was hierarchical, its underlying spirit was that of 'interdependence' among different caste groups. There were differences, but interdependence united the village community. Reciprocity implied, explicitly or implicitly, an exchange of equal services and non-exploitative relations. Mutual gratification was supposed to be the outcome of reciprocal exchange. As Wiser explained, 'Each serves the other. Each in turn is master. Each in turn is servant' (1969: 10).

The later studies carried out during the 1950s and 1960s were much more elaborate and contained long descriptions of different forms of social inequalities and differences in rural society. However, many of them also continued to use the framework of reciprocity and functional integration. Relations of caste too were approached from a similar kind of perspective. For many of them, caste was the most critical social institution in rural India and 'determined and decided all social relations'. However, the field-view did capture some obvious complexities of the ground situation. For example, though the institution of caste existed in different parts of the subcontinent, the framework of varna that arranged groups in an order with Brahmins at the top and untouchables at the bottom was only partly correct. In principle, caste was a closed system where 'entry into a social status was a function of heredity and not of individual achievement' (Majumdar: 1958: 19). However, the way caste operated at the local level was quite different from the way in which the varna scheme expressed it. Mutual rank was uncertain and arguable. By implication, 'mobility was possible in caste' (Srinivas 1976: 175). Srinivas developed the concept of Sanskritization to show that the system of caste hierarchies was after all not so rigid and closed as it appeared from the 'book-view'. He used the term 'Sanskritization' to describe the process of group mobility within the ritual order of hierarchy and characterized it as a

... process by which a 'low' Hindu caste, or tribal or other group, changes its customs, ritual, ideology, and way of life in the direction of a high and frequently, 'twice-born' caste. Generally such changes are followed by a claim to higher position in the caste hierarchy than that traditionally conceded to the claimant caste by the local community. (Srinivas 1972: 6)

While ritual and religious traditions largely shaped the social framework of rural life, secular factors, such as landownership, also played their role. Srinivas underlined this point in the following words:

The articulated criteria of ranking were usually ritual, religious or moral resulting in concealing the importance of secular criteria. The influence of the latter was, however, real. For instance, while landownership and numerical strength were crucial in improving caste rank, any claim to high rank had to be expressed in ritual and symbolic terms. (Srinivas 1976: 176)

Elsewhere, he also argues that it was difficult for an 'untouchable' caste to resort to group mobility through Sanskitization, primarily because 'untouchables in Rampura were either landless laborers, tenants, or very small landowners', and with very little engagement with education (Srinivas 1959: 3). Similarly, when Dube identified factors that contributed towards the status differentiation in the village community of Shamirpet, along with caste and religion, he also counted land-ownership, wealth, position in government service and village organization, age, and distinctive personality traits (Dube 1955: 161). Similarly, stressing the secular functions of caste, Dube pointed out that at times the caste panchayats of the menials worked as unions to secure their employment and strengthen their bargaining power vis-à-vis the landowning dominant castes.

While the social anthropologists questioned the colonial and orientalist notion of caste derived from the book-view, they accepted the idea that the 'Indian village' is a representative of the authentic native life. However, the notion of Indian society being a land of 'village-republics' was itself a colonial construct, where caste appeared to be the natural frame of social organization. Along with the earlier writings of James Mill, Charles Metcalfe's notion of the Indian village community set the tone for much of the later writings on rural India. Metcalfe, in his celebrated remark stated that 'the Indian village communities were little republics, having nearly everything they wanted within themselves, and almost independent of foreign relations. They seemed to last where nothing else lasted. Dynasty after dynasty tumbled down; revolution succeeded revolution but the village community remained the same' (as quoted in Cohn 1987: 213) His idea of the caste system based on the notion of interdependence was central to this notion of the Indian village.

The nationalist leadership of the Indian freedom movement also accepted the colonial construct of the 'Indian village' as a given fact, and to a significant extent, it shaped their understanding of traditional Indian life (Jodhka 2002a). The village came to be widely viewed as a representative of authentic native life. For example, though Gandhi was careful to not glorify the decaying village of British India, he nevertheless celebrated the so-called simplicity and authenticity of village life, an image largely derived from colonial representations of the Indian village.

The social anthropologists uncritically accepted this simplistic construct of the Indian village and its social order of caste. Thus, notwithstanding the differences of perspective and method, they continued to approach caste as 'tradition', which, like the Indian village, had been around for ages. Even when it allowed some changes, like Sanskritization, its structural and moral frame remained intact. Not only did they view caste as being quintessentially a fact of traditional village life, they also, quite like the orientalists, viewed it as a part of Hindu social and ritual life.

They all accepted the colonial constructs of Indian society as given historical facts about the Indian society. They all seem to share the underlying assumption that India was a land of religion and rituals, of caste and Hinduism, inimical to change and outside influence.

However, given that the village studies produced detailed descriptive accounts of rural social life, they also presented caste relations as they observed them. Interestingly, a closer reading of some of these studies provides us with a different picture of caste relations where power and domination are central to its every-day reproduction. The next chapter looks at caste as power and begins with a descriptive account of caste as presented by the social anthropologists in studies of the 'traditional' Indian village.

2

Caste as Power

... traditionally Brahmins did not have much direct
connection with Adi-Dravidas. They gave their land
to Non-Brahmin tenants who, in their turn engaged
Adi-Dravida labourers. In other ways also Brahmins
were often dependent on Non-Brahmins for dealing
with Adi-Dravidas. When an Adi-Dravida misbehaved,
a Brahmin *mirasdar* might ask his Non-Brahmin
tenant to fetch the miscreant from the *cheri*, tie him
to a tree, and give him a beating. Physical force ... was
one of the most effective sanctions against the Adi-
Dravidas ... (Béteille 1996: 168)

The classical view of caste, as we have seen in the previous chapter, is that it has been a part of the Indian
tradition, embedded in Hindu religion. Tradition, in
this view, is a static given, which remained virtually

unchanged for centuries. The 'traditional' institutions like the village and caste began to change, initially during the colonial period under Western influence, and later with the process of development and democratization introduced after independence.

This view, in a sense, continues to prevail. However, the recent, and not so recent, social scientific research on the subject and the popular social movements around caste have frequently questioned the validity of such an understanding of caste. Today, different people talk about caste in different ways and voices. The most commonly invoked categories in relation to caste, or along with caste, in the popular and academic discourses, are those of 'power' and 'politics'.

As indicated in the previous chapter, many scholars have questioned the theoretical validity of the classical argument that in Indian society 'status' was derived from religious ideology, and that it worked independently of the economic and political realities or the structures of power and domination in the Indian society. The orientalist scholarship also underlined the point that the Hindus *valued* 'status' more than material wealth or power and, therefore, within the caste society of India, status was superior to the worldly positions achieved through acquisition of material wealth and/or control over institutions of dominance.

However, one could easily argue that such a division was only an imaginary formulation. 'Hierarchy' and 'status' are also dimensions or forms of 'power'. The fact that status in India had religious connotations does not mean that its experience as a relationship was in any way different from the experience of power and inequality. Moreover, its reproduction in everyday life would have been possible only through operation of 'power', coercive or legitimate (including religious ideology).

'Caste as power' is no new formulation. Sociologists, social anthropologists, and other social scientists have extensively explored the 'power' dimension of caste. The subject of caste remained a major preoccupation with sociologists and social anthropologists during the 1950s and 1960s when they carried out intensive field-based studies of the Indian village society. These were invariably based on prolonged fieldwork, carried out by an individual scholar in a single village by staying with the 'community'. The social anthropologists had brought the method of 'participant observation' to the study of the Indian village from their earlier experience

35

of studying small tribal communities. Though many of them worked with the category of the Indian village quite uncritically borrowed from the earlier orientalist constructs of India, they also reported what they observed on ground in a matter-of-fact manner and caste invariably appeared as a coercive power relationship in these accounts.

The social anthropologists who studied the village social life used categories like the 'dominant caste' as useful descriptive tools. Some of these empirical studies also drew conceptual inferences and theorized the ritual universe of caste in terms of power relationships.

Caste, power, and politics are also subjects of contemporary relevance. Perhaps the most frequent use of the word 'caste' today takes place in the context of democratic and electoral politics. From the lay public to the psephologists of popular media, and serious academic analysts, almost everyone treats caste as an important variable influencing the working of the democratic political process in India. As popular presumption goes, caste communities determine electoral outcomes; they work as pressure groups and influence governance agenda of the Indian state at the local, regional and national levels. Several political parties have been formed around caste-based identities, and for such parties, caste considerations shape political programmes, leaderships, and ideologies.

This chapter begins with a short introduction to sociological accounts of the relationship between caste and power in 'traditional' rural settings. This is followed by a brief discussion on some of the theoretical literature that looks at caste as a relationship of power. Finally, the chapter provides a broad understanding of how social scientists in India have engaged with the question of 'caste and democratic politics'.

Caste, Power, and Dominance

The most obvious empirical reference point of the traditional Indian social formation is the village. Along with caste, village was also seen as a signifier of the traditional social life in India. The 'village studies' carried out by sociologists and social anthropologists during the 1950s and 1960s were mostly uncritical of the then popular orientalist categories and theoretical frameworks. A close reading of these accounts, however, clearly shows that caste in everyday life was lived as a relationship of power and its reproduction often required the use of coercive means. It may be useful to begin with a discussion of the concept of 'dominant caste', popularized by the well-known Indian sociologist, M.N. Srinivas. Elaborating on the concept while presenting his 'field–view' of the Indian village, Srinivas, wrote: 'A caste may be said to be 'dominant' when it preponderates numerically over the other castes, and when it also wields preponderant economic and political power. A large and powerful caste group can be more easily dominant if its position in the local caste hierarchy is not too low' (Srinivas 1955: 18).

In a later paper, he added that another element of dominance was becoming increasingly important in rural India, namely, the number of educated persons in a caste and the occupations they pursue. Villagers were aware of the importance of this criterion. They would like their young men to be educated and to be officers in the Government (Srinivas 1959: 1). Perhaps the most interesting aspect of Srinivas's discussion on the subject is that he describes the power dimension of caste relations quite vividly, completely free from the Dumontian preoccupation with the idea of 'caste' as being purely 'status'. For Srinivas, the ritual status of a given caste was not only essential for it to become dominant but it was itself a feature, or a dimension, of dominance. As he writes, while trying to elaborate what he observed in his village: '... the different elements of dominance are distributed among the castes in a village. Thus a caste which is ritually high may be poor and lacking strength in numbers, while a populous caste may be poor and ritually low' (1959: 2).

Even when the 'ritual dominance existed by itself, unaccompanied by the other forms of dominance', it had to be supported by material prosperity.

> ... the Brahmin priest of the Rama temple and the Lingayat priests of the Madeshwara and Basava temples, are quite well off by village standards. The main source of income for these families is from the land with which the temples have been endowed, while a subsidiary but not unimportant source is the gifts in cash or kind which the devotees make to the priests whenever they visit the temples or during harvest. (Ibid.: 3)

Perhaps the most important point that Srinivas makes in relation to caste and dominance is the

dynamics of the relationship between the two aspects
of rural life:

> ... when a caste enjoys one form of dominance, it
> is frequently able to acquire the other forms as well
> in course of time. Thus a caste which is numerically
> strong and wealthy will be able to move up in the ritual
> hierarchy if it Sanskritizes its ritual and way of life, and
> also loudly and persistently proclaims itself to be what
> it wants to be. It is hardly necessary to add that the
> more forms of dominance which a caste enjoys, the
> easier it is for it to acquire the rest. (Ibid.: 3)

Srinivas also indicates quite clearly that untouchability was about control over the lives of untouchables,
a relationship of power (like slavery), reinforced with
coercion, if required. For example, he quotes an instance
of the decision of some local untouchable communities in the village he was studying, to 'give up perform-
ing services such as removing the carcasses of dead
cattle from the houses of the higher castes, beating the
tom-tom at the festivals of village deities, and removing
the leaves on which the high castes had dined during
festivals and weddings' (Ibid.: 3–4). This annoyed the
Bihalli peasants and they '... beat up the Untouchables

and set fire to their huts. A similar attempt by the Kere Untouchables was nipped in the bud by the local Peasants. The dominant caste of Peasants in Rampura is plainly opposed to the emancipation of Untouchables' (Ibid.: 4).

Another classic study of a south Indian village by André Béteille presents the relationship of caste, ritual traditions, and domination in the village society even more sharply. Ritual status was not independent of power but one of its core dimensions. Based on his long-drawn fieldwork in a village in the Tanjore district of Tamil Nadu, he writes:

> Up to the 1940s the Brahmins enjoyed a great measure of power in the village. Their power was based upon ownership of land, *high social and ritual status*, and superior education ... The *panchayat* president was a Brahmin, the *panchayat* room was in the *agraharam*, and initiative in all important matters was in the hands of Brahmins ... Non-Brahmin members ... had the position of second-class citizens. (1996: 152, emphasis added)

As was the case with the village that M.N. Srinivas studied, use of coercive violence to 'discipline' the

41

untouchables was a common practice of hierarchical power, which kept the three sets of caste communities, the Brahmins, the Dravidas (middle-level peasants), and the Adi-Dravidas (the untouchables) tied to each other (Ibid.: 168).

F.G. Bailey who studied a village in eastern India also underlined the coercive nature of the inter-caste relationship. He even questioned the idea of interdependence in caste society, as he wrote: 'The system works the way it does because the coercive sanctions are all in the hands of a dominant caste. There is a tie of reciprocity, but it is not a sanction of which the dependent castes can make easy use' (Bailey 1960: 258).

Fluid Status of the Brahmin

An important conclusion of the discussion above is that though the Brahmins enjoyed high status in the village setting, it was largely because of their overall economic strength, particularly their ownership of land. However, in some other regions of the subconti-nent, the Brahmins did not enjoy high status because they did not own agricultural land. Perhaps the most interesting example in this context is the northwestern region of Punjab.

Writing on the social life in colonial Punjab, Prakash Tandon, in his celebrated autobiographical work, *Punjabi Century*, observes that the Brahmins of Punjab lived a 'frugal life' and it was rare to find 'an affluent Brahmin' in the region (Tandon 1961: 77). Most Brahmins in his native village were treated as members of the menial castes. Like other menials, they too were mostly dependent upon the food they collected from their *jajman*s. Giving a vivid description of their social status, he writes:

> With us, brahmins were an underprivileged class and exercised little or no influence on the community.
>
> Our brahmins did not as a rule even have the role of teachers, because until the British opened regular schools, teaching was done by Muslim mullahs in the mosques or by Sikh *granthis* ... in the Gurudwaras. Our brahmins were rarely erudite; in fact many of them were barely literate, possessing only a perfunctory knowledge of rituals and knowing just the necessary mantras by heart. (Ibid.: 1961: 76)

Similarly, Satish Saberwal, a well-known social anthropologist who studied a small town of Punjab during the late 1960s, writes: '... even if the Brahmins were able to carve a ceremonial place at Ranjit Singh's court for themselves, there is no evidence that they acquired much land or that they were able to enforce the social circumstances that they would have required for maintaining high levels of ritual purity' (1976: 7).

Commenting on the absence of any kind of reverence for the Brahmins in Punjab, Saberwal quotes Chanana: 'In Punjabi the word *Pandat* (Pandit) denotes a Brahman and may connote some respect for the latter. But the word *Bahman* (Brahmin) almost always carries a little contempt' (Ibid.: 10).

Scholars have also observed rural–urban differences in the nature of caste hierarchies in northwest India. While in urban Punjab, the Khatris and Aroras (trading castes) were considered as the most superior communities, in rural Punjab and Haryana, the landowning Jats were supreme and they did not consider anyone above them. Brahmins themselves tended to concede to such a framework of ranking (D'Souza 1967).

Researchers on caste also reported the absence of a common framework across caste groups on the nature of hierarchy or the positions that different groups ought to occupy. The so-called ideological framework of caste and the varna model are contested and disputed categories, a subject to be discussed in more detail in the next chapter.

Theorizing Caste as Power

The classical orientalist writings, including the Dumontian version, also provide a larger framework for understanding the Indian/Hindu society and its difference from the modern societies of the West. Unlike the modern West, the essence of Indian culture lay in its religious principles. The supremacy of the 'religious principle', articulated in the form of oppositional unity of the pure and impure (as in Dumont), also meant that in India, the secular domain of power was independent of the religious domain, and inferior to it. That is how Dumont establishes the supremacy of the Brahmin in Indian society. Raheja puts it quite sharply:

> The most pervasive and persistent Western view of Hindu society sees hierarchy as the sole ideology defining relations among castes. In this narrow view, caste is seen as focused on the Brahman value of purity, while the king and the dominant caste... are taken to represent only a residual, devalued, and

45

non-ideological sphere of 'political' and 'economic' relations. (1989: 79)

A range of scholars have questioned this formulation on various grounds. Some scholars have also tried to construct alternative theories. Here we briefly discuss the works of Nicholas Dirks and Gloria Goodwin Raheja.

Based on his extensive historical work on caste practices and ethnographic studies of Kallars in Tamil Nadu, Nicholas Dirks offers a critique of Dumont and an alternative conceptualization of caste in his book *Castes of Mind*. Dirks, for example, convincingly shows how the colonial rulers through a process of enumeration and ethnographic surveys raised consciousness about caste. They also produced social and intellectual conditions where 'caste became the single term capable of expressing, organizing, and above all "synthesizing" India's diverse forms of social identity, community and organization' (Dirks 2001: 5).

The 'Original Caste', as he argues in the book as well as in another essay on the subject, was a diverse reality and did not follow any one single principle, as suggested by Dumont. He questions Dumont's central assumption about the separation of religious authority and political power in the Indian/Hindu society. While Dumont recognizes that the king is all-powerful in the secular domain, his power was inferior to the religious authority of the Brahmin, 'articulated in terms of the opposition of purity and impurity' (Dirks 1989: 59). This, Dirks argues, was not the case in Tamil Nadu. There was 'no fundamental ontological separation of a "religious" from a "political" domain'. Religious institutions and the domain of power (of the king) were completely meshed with each other. The king drew his power from religious worship. For status or religion to encompass power, they had to be separate realities. This, Dirk argues, was not the case in reality. It will be useful to present his argument in his own words:

> ... temples represent the pre-eminent position of the king by granting him the highest honour in the temple, before even the learned ... Brahmin. Religion does not encompass kingship any more than kingship encompasses religion. There are not two distinct forms of power ... King and Brahmin are both privileged but by different forms of divinity in a world in which all beings were ... generated from the same ontological source ... (Ibid.: 61)

Richard Burghart also put forth a similar argument based on his study of the Hindu kingdom of Nepal. Not only were there no doubts about the supremacy of the king in the Hindu kingdom of Nepal, but the Brahmin had also been incorporated into civic administration, which effectively made the Brahmin a servant of the kingdom. The king was also not a mere political head. He also 'deified the kingship'.

> The king magnified his stature by identifying himself with the deities of the various sectarian cults. In … his role as the Protector of the Earth the king identified himself with the god Vishnu. The king of Nepal is said to be an incarnation of Vishnu … like many of the former Rajput kings of western India …'
> (Burghart 1978: 528)

While Dirks and Burghart focused on macro structures of power and the kingship to show that 'divinity' and 'power' were not two separate spheres in the so-called traditional Indian society, G.G. Raheja studied a micro setting in north India and found the Brahmin-centric notion of caste as being completely misleading. Though caste divisions existed in the region, she questioned the assumption that there was one single underlying value system or ideology that shaped caste relations everywhere. On the contrary: '... there are several contextually shifting ideologies of inter-caste relationships apparent in everyday village social life. Meanings and values are foregrounded differently from context to context, and they implicate varying configurations of castes ...' (Raheja 1989: 81).

Raheja provides a completely different interpretation of ritual life in rural India through her study of a Uttar Pradesh village. One of the core features of caste relations in her village that determined the place and status of different caste groups was the patterns of gift-giving and receiving (presentations, or *len–den,* as understood in the local language). Instead of looking at caste from the perspective of hierarchy, she tried to understand the relationship through the categories of 'centrality' and 'mutuality'.

The dominant caste group in the village, the Gujars, always occupied the central place in the jajmani system and their relationship with the Brahmins and the Kamins (the servicing castes) was that of 'mutuality'. Among other things, the relationship among them was also governed by a ritual order of presentations, len–den.

Dan (gift) giving and receiving is an important activity in the cultural life of the village, 'throughout the yearly cycle of seasons and festivals, and throughout the life course, as well as when specific afflictions and troubles have beset a family or the village as a whole' (Ibid.: 82). Those who give dan do so for promoting their own well-being, personal or collective. However, dan also involves transferring 'evil (*pap*), affliction (*kasht*), fault (*dosh*), and inauspiciousness more generally'. When dan is given and received in a ritual context, the negativity (inauspiciousness) comes out of the donor, and is transferred to the recipient, along with the dan.

The relationship of dan-giving and dan-receiving is central to the manner in which caste relationships are structured in the north Indian village. While different caste groups give dan on various ritual occasions, the Gujars do it the most. More importantly, while other caste groups in the jajmani system have to also receive dan (a ritual obligation), being the dominant caste, Gujars are the only ones who do not do so, and this is a symbolic signifier of their overall dominance, material and ritual. In her village, Raheja argues,

... Gujar dominance is absolute. They comprise slightly more than one-half of the total population, but they hold virtually all of the land. They are regarded as the *jajmans* not only with respect to their own domestic and agricultural rituals, but also in relation to the ritual life of the village as a unit ... (1989: 98)

Dominance is not simply a matter of a caste's numerical preponderance or the 'temporal' aspect of landholding. Though landholding and numerical preponderance may in fact ... be necessary conditions ... it is the sacrificial function, the giving away and dispersal of evil and inauspiciousness for the well-being and prosperity of the village that is seen by all castes ... as the fulcrum of dominance and of *jajmani* relationships in the village. (Ibid.: 98–9)

Interestingly, Dirks and Raheja are not the only ones to point to the possibility of multiple and competing interpretations of caste relations. A large volume of literature produced by scholars working on the 'untouchables' similarly shows that interpretations of caste from 'below' rarely go along with those offered from the 'above', a point to be discussed in detail in the next chapter.

Caste and Politics in Contemporary India

The leaders of India's freedom movement did not have a uniform attitude towards caste. While Gandhi found nothing fundamentally wrong with the system of caste-based divisions in the Indian society, leaders like Nehru, Ambedkar and most others from the Western-educated middle class were openly critical of the caste system and argued that it should have no place in modern democratic India. It is the latter view that appears to have shaped the vision of the Indian Constitution on the subject of caste.

Articulating the then 'mainstream' position on the subject among the middle-class elite of the country in his well-known book *The Discovery of India,* Pandit Jawaharlal Nehru, India's first Prime Minister wrote in 1946:

> In the context of society today, the caste system and much that goes with it are wholly incompatible, reactionary, restrictive, and barriers to progress. There can be no equality in status and opportunity within its framework, nor can there be political democracy... Between these two conceptions conflict is inherent and only one of them can survive. (1946: 257)

The Chairman of India's Constituent Assembly and the first Law Minister of independent India, B.R. Ambedkar, was even more emphatic on this. He wrote: 'You cannot build anything on the foundations of caste. You cannot build up a nation; you cannot build up a morality. Anything you will build on the foundations of caste will crack and will never be a whole' (2002: 102).

The opening pages of the Indian Constitution, its Preamble, envisaged a nation where the values of equality, liberty, and fraternity would be supreme. Drawn mostly from the historical experience and cultural traditions of the West, these ideas reflected a vision of a liberal democracy and a modern society that were to ensure a dignified existence to each and every individual and endow them with certain fundamental rights vis-à-vis the state and fellow citizens. They contradicted very fundamentally the spirit of caste and hierarchy as principles of social organization. The Directive Principles of State Policy (Article 38) of the Indian Constitution made it further clear by explicitly stating that 'The State shall strive to promote the welfare of the people by securing and protecting as effectively as it may a social order in which justice, social, economic and political, shall inform all the institutions of national life' (as quoted in Shah 2002: 2).

Any form of discrimination on grounds of religion, race, caste, gender, or place of birth was made punishable by law.

Following the practices in democratic regimes of the Western world, the Indian Constitution invested all legislative powers in certain institutions of governance, to be made up of elected representatives of the Indian people. Representatives to these bodies were to be chosen strictly following the principle of universal adult franchise.

While the middle-class leaders of independent India decried caste, they did not simply take a moral position against this 'traditional' institution. The 'mainstream' Indian political leadership recognized the 'crippling' impact that the working of the system over the centuries would have had on the subordinated sections of the Indian people and the implications of this 'ancient' system for building a true democracy and individual citizenship. It was to address these concerns that the Indian Constitution instituted certain legal and institutional measures, albeit temporarily, to enable groups and communities of people who had been historically disadvantaged in the given social system, to participate in the game of democratic politics on equal terms (Galanter 1984).

There will be little dispute on the positive effects of the Indian policies and programmes of affirmative action in enabling the historically deprived sections of Indian people to participate in the economic and political life of the nation. India has also been exceptionally successful in having been able to institutionalize a healthy system of democratic governance at different levels of its political system. However, while these achievements are certainly commendable, it has not meant an end of caste in the social or political life of the nation. In fact, many would argue that politically caste is a much more active institution today than it ever was in the past and it is largely thanks to the electoral processes and competitive politics. Though it may appear that the democratic and electoral experience has belied the hopes of the founders of the modern nation, the survival of caste, or its increased involvement with politics, is no reflection on the working of democracy in India or an evidence of its failure. The available literature on electoral systems and other aspects of political life clearly points towards a process that has been described by Indian political scientists as a deepening of democracy (see Yadav 1999; Palshikar 2004), and it becoming more inclusive of social groups and categories of the Indian population (Jayal 2001). How does one make sense of this apparently contradictory reality?

Caste and Democratic Politics

Notwithstanding their personal predispositions towards a liberal view of democratic politics and faith in evolutionist notions of social change, the inevitability of the Western style of modernization, or their preoccupation with categories inherited from colonial and orientalist writings on India, social anthropologists recognized the tremendous resilience that the institution of caste was showing on the ground.

Quite early on they had begun to report on the likely impact that caste could have on the working of 'modern' institutions, and in turn the implications of a new form of politics for the system of caste hierarchy. For example, some of them were quick to recognize the fact that instead of completely replacing the traditional 'ascriptive structures' of caste society by an open system of social stratification based on individual choice and

achievement, new modes of governance and growing use of modern technology could in some ways
strengthen caste, while weakening its structural logic.

Commenting on the nature of change being experienced in caste with the rise of non-Brahmin movements in the southern provinces, G.S. Ghurye had
argued as early as in 1932 that attack on hierarchy by
such mobilizations did not necessarily mean the end
of caste. These mobilizations generated a new kind of
collective sentiment, 'the feeling of caste solidarity'
which could be 'truly described as caste patriotism'
(1932: 192).

M.N. Srinivas developed this point further in his
writings during the late 1950s. Focusing specifically on
the possible consequences of modern technology and
representational politics, both of which were introduced by the colonial rulers in India, he argued that far
from disappearing with the process of modernization,
caste was experiencing a 'horizontal consolidation'.
Commenting on the impact of modern technology on
caste, he wrote:

> The coming in of printing, of a regular postal service,
> of vernacular newspapers and books, of the telegraph,

railway and bus, enabled the representatives of a caste living in different areas to meet and discuss their common problems and interests. Western education gave new political values such as liberty and equality. The educated leaders started caste journals and held caste conferences. Funds were collected to organize the caste, and to help the poorer members. Caste hostels, hospitals, co-operative societies etc., became a common feature of urban social life. In general it may be confidently said that the last hundred years have seen a great increase in caste solidarity, and the concomitant decrease of a sense of interdependence between different castes living in a region. (Srinivas 1962: 74–5)

Similarly, the introduction of certain kinds of representational politics by the British helped in this process of horizontal consolidation of caste.

The policy which the British adopted of giving a certain amount of power to local self-governing bodies, and preferences and concessions to backward castes provided new opportunities to castes. In order to be able to take advantage of these opportunities, caste groups, as traditionally understood, entered into alliances with each other to form bigger entities. (Ibid.: 5)

However, this was not a one-way process. The caste system too was undergoing a change. The horizontal solidarity of caste, which also meant a kind of 'competition' among different castes at the politico-economic plane, eventually weakened the vertical solidarity of caste (Srinivas 1962: 74; Bailey 1963). This process received a further impetus with the introduction of democratic politics after India's independence.

Challenged with the question of change in caste order, Louis Dumont too followed Srinivas and speculated on similar lines. Castes, he argued, did not disappear with the process of economic and political change, but its logic was altered 'from a fluid, structural universe in which the emphasis is on interdependence ... to a universe of improbable blocks ... essentially identical and in competition ... as a substance' (1998: 222).

These attempts at theorizations of the changing realities of caste opened up many new possibilities for looking at the dynamic relationship of caste with the democratic political process. Thus by the 1960s, sociologists and political scientists began to talk about caste and politics in a different language. Discussions shifted from a predominantly moral or normative concern about the 'corruption' that caste brought into the democratic political process to more empirical processes of interaction between caste and democratic politics. The gradual institutionalization of democratic politics changed caste equations. Power shifted from one set of caste groups, the so-called ritually purer upper castes, to middle-level 'dominant castes'. Democratic politics also introduced a process of differentiation at the local levels of power structure. As Béteille reported in his study of a village in Tamil Nadu during the late 1960s: '... a vast body of new structures of power has emerged in India since Independence. Today traditional bodies such as groups of caste elders (which are functionally diffuse) have to compete increasingly with functionally specific structures of power such as parties and statutory panchayats' (1970: 246–7).

However, this differentiation did not mean that these new structures were free of caste. Caste soon featured in their working but the authority of these institutions had to be reproduced differently. Though traditional sources of power continued to be relevant, introduction of universal adult franchise also made 'numbers' of individual caste communities in a given local setting crucial. Power could be reproduced only through mobilization, vertically as well as horizontally. This also gave birth to a new class of political entrepreneurs. Over the years some of them have begun to work successfully, often going beyond a single caste-cluster for mobilizing a political constituency, thus undermining the logic of caste politics (Krishna 2001).

Caste Associations

While sociologists and social anthropologists talked about horizontal consolidation of castes or its substantialization into 'ethnic communities', political sociologists worked on the phenomenon and possible roles of caste associations in democratic politics. Beginning with the late nineteenth century, different parts of the subcontinent saw the emergence of 'caste associations'. While on the face of it, caste associations appeared like a typical case of Indian tradition trying to assert itself against the modernizing tendencies unleashed by the colonial rule, they, in fact, represented a different kind of process. Lloyd Rudolf and Susan Rudolf were among the first to study the phenomenon of caste associations in democratic India. They looked at caste associations as agents of modernity in a traditional society like India and argued that the caste association was

> ... no longer an ascriptive association in the sense in which caste taken as jati was and is. It has taken on features of a voluntary association. Membership in caste association is *not* purely ascriptive; birth in the caste is a necessary but not a sufficient condition for membership. One must also *join* through some conscious act involving various degrees of identification ... (1967: 33, emphasis original)

Through his study *The Nadars of Tamilnad* (1969), Robert Hardgrave further reinforced their thesis by arguing that the caste association of Nadars worked like a pressure group and had played an important role in the upward social mobility of the community. M.N. Srinivas (1966) too similarly argued that caste associations came up as agents of social mobility for the caste communities at the time when British rulers introduced enumeration of castes.

Rajni Kothari also argued more or less on similar lines while writing on caste and the democratic political process in India. In the introduction to the celebrated volume *Caste in Indian Politics* (1970) that he edited, Kothari argued against the popular notion that democratic politics was helping traditional institutions like caste to 'resuscitate and re-establish their legitimacy'. This could lead to 'disintegrative tendencies' and could potentially 'disrupt the democratic and secular framework of Indian polity'. In reality, however,

> ... the consequences of caste-politics interactions are just the reverse of what is usually stated. It is not politics that gets caste-ridden; it is caste that gets politicised. Dialectical as it might sound, it is precisely because the operation of competitive politics has drawn caste out of its apolitical context and given it a new status that the 'caste system' as hitherto known has eroded and has begun to disintegrate ... (Kothari 1970: 20–1)

The caste federation, he argued,

> once formed on the basis of caste identities ... goes on to acquire non-caste functions, becomes more flexible in organisation as time passes, even begins to accept members and leaders from castes other than those with which it started, stretches out to new regions, and also makes common cause with other voluntary organisations, interest groups and political parties. In course of time, the federation becomes a distinctly political group. (Ibid.: 21–2)

Speaking in a less enthusiastic language, Ghanshyam Shah also made a similar point. Though in the long run caste associations did promote competitive politics and participation, they also exacerbated parochialism, he argued (Shah 1975).

Notwithstanding the deviation they brought into the process of democratic politics as understood in the classical Western textbooks on democracy, caste associations did play a role in spreading the culture of democratic politics in areas that were hitherto governed exclusively by tradition. As argued by Arnold et al.:

> The caste association was a social adapter, improvised to connect two sets of social and political forms. It helped to reconcile the values of traditional society with those of a new order by continuing to use caste as the basis for social organization, but at the same time introducing new objectives—education and supra-local political power ... (1976: 372)

In their comparative study of caste associations in different parts of south India they found that, interestingly, leaders of these associations did not come from 'the traditional caste authorities but from the most enterprising of the misfits—the Western educated, the lawyers, the urban businessmen, the retired government servants. These men were few in number; but they looked back over their shoulders, hoping that the rest of their community supported them and would help the misfits to establish themselves more firmly in their non-traditional careers' (Ibid.: 372).

Though caste associations have continued to be important actors in politics and in the community life of Indian citizens, social science research interest in the subject declined during the ensuing decades. The popular belief that caste shapes democratic politics in India has also continued to prevail. The introduction of the Mandal Commission Report, which had recommended quotas for the Other Backward Classes (OBCs) as well, by the Central Government in 1991, further reinforced the presence of the caste-idiom in democratic politics. Though quotas for the OBCs had already been in place in several states of India, the acceptance of the Mandal Commission Report offered a new kind of legitimacy to caste-based mobilizations.

More importantly perhaps, the process of democratization gradually spread downwards. Until the late 1980s, caste politics and the politics of caste had largely remained confined to the middle-level caste groups, who owned agricultural lands, and were large in numbers, the typical regional level dominant castes. Those who were below the 'line of pollution', the ex-untouchable communities, had until then participated in democratic politics mostly through patron structures of the so-called national parties, dominated by the so-called upper castes. By the late 1980s a new middle-class elite had emerged from within these communities, which started articulating the concerns of these socially excluded communities from within, and in a different language.

A new perspective on caste thus began to emerge from below. Though B.R. Ambedkar had already provided a powerful articulation of the 'untouchable' voice, it had remained peripheral to the mainstream political discourses until the 1980s. The new political elite from the ex-untouchable communities resurrected Ambedkar and his mission through the idea of 'Dalit' politics. The term 'Dalit', meaning 'the broken, ground-down, downtrodden, or oppressed', has its origins in the political movements in Maharashtra, first used in the context of caste oppression by the nineteenth-century reformer, Jyotiba Phule (Mendelsohn and Vicziany 2000: 5). It was introduced as part of this new language as the most preferable category of self-description by several different ex-untouchable communities and individuals across the subcontinent. Dalit perspectives on caste have acquired wide currency over the last two decades and are discussed in the following chapter.

3

Caste as Humiliation

When someone says 'I am a Jat', his chest expands.
But when we say 'Chamar', we contract to nothing.
(A Scheduled Caste student in conversation with a
sociologist, Aggarwal 1983: 24)

The Hindu, a national daily, reported on 8 May 2011 a
case of suicide by a Dalit student in a medical college
in Chandigarh in northwest India. He was in the final
year and had been 'an excellent student throughout'.
He had failed in the relatively 'easy' subject of community medicine. Tragically, when three other teach-
ers evaluated his script, they found his answer script
good enough and passed him. He became a doctor,
but posthumously. The teacher concerned had failed
him because the upper-caste teacher could not accept

the idea of an 'untouchable' person becoming a doctor. The teacher, who was also Head of the Department, reportedly told him that 'he might have entered medical college using his Scheduled Caste certificate but he would not go out with a degree'.

This was certainly not a rare or unique case. Human rights activists working on caste-related questions reported several such cases from different parts of India during the year 2010–11. However, in most cases, the violence is more direct, invariably in reaction to the growing aspiration for a life of dignity among the members and communities of India's ex-untouchables. One does not have to search in libraries for stories of caste-related violence against the ex-untouchables. The reports of caste-related atrocities come from every corner of the country where caste has been in practice, and they come almost daily, even in twenty-first-century India.

More importantly for us, the frequent reports of caste violence raise questions of wider theoretical and practical/political significance. What is the nature of caste-related violence? Is there a pattern across regions of contemporary India? What are the implications of such incidents for social relations across caste communities?

How does it transform the nature of caste identities? How far do the theoretical writings discussed in the previous chapter help us understand untouchability and caste violence? We try to find answers to these questions in this chapter.

Caste System and the Line of Pollution

Viewed from 'below', the most critical feature of caste is the experience of untouchability. The line of pollution, which divided the 'untouchables' from the rest, has been historically a critical point of distinction. The idea of the 'line of pollution' has also been an important category in the official discourse on caste. In most cases it was used as the boundary line for identifying the 'Scheduled Castes' (SCs) and for institutionalizing policies of affirmative action for their 'welfare'. This administrative classification and grouping of different caste communities has, over the years, begun to shape the popular notions of caste and caste-related distinctions in social and political life.

In some sense, the idea of untouchability is an obvious extension of the idea of pollution, or of the notion of purity and impurity. However, untouchability is also much more than what the notion of pollution suggests. Nowhere in the line of hierarchy is the rigidity of caste as sharp as it is around the line of pollution. For example, for those above the line of pollution, including those designated as Shudras, in the traditional scriptural system of hierarchy, impurity was relative. As shown by empirical studies of village life (see Chapter 1), those above the line of pollution could contest their position in ranking order, either through the use of force and power or by gradually Sanskritizing themselves by adopting the lifestyle of those considered above them. However, for those located below the line of pollution, the so-called untouchable communities, impurity was absolute. Only rarely could it be overcome within the framework of tradition. The path of social mobility through Sanskritization was not available to the untouchables. Only rarely could an 'untouchable' community move up and overcome their 'low' status while living within the framework of tradition. For them, caste indeed was a closed system of inequality.

However, notwithstanding its critical importance in the traditional system of hierarchy, the idea of the line

71

of pollution does not appear to have had a very long history. For example, its scriptural confirmation is only vague. An English translation of a passage from Manu's text states: 'The Brahmana, the Kshatriya and the Vaisya castes (varna) are the twice-born ones, but the fourth, the Sudra, has one birth only; there is no fifth (caste)' (*The Laws of Manu* X, 4 Buhler 1886, quoted in Charsley 1996: 3).

It took several years of deliberations, among the colonial administrators and the social and religious reformers of the late nineteenth/early twentieth century to work out the conceptual distinction. The early colonial administrators who had developed their understanding of the Indian society and caste system from scriptural sources, found it hard to make sense of untouchability when they were confronted by its practice, particularly when it came to enumerating caste. The *chatur* (four)-varna model of hierarchy was not of much help. Distinguishing between Shudras and untouchables was empirically critical but conceptually difficult with the varna model. The colonial literature remained preoccupied with the varna system of hierarchy and the challenge was to place the untouchable into the model.

Simon Charsley argues that it was through the consistent efforts of Herbert Risley, who was also the Commissioner of the 1901 Census, that the term untouchability, as we understand it today, came to be recognized in the colonial administrative discourse (Charsley 1996). Risley tried to deal with the question by subdividing the Shudras into four different hierarchical categories on the basis of their polluting effect. The untouchables were at the bottom of this hierarchy and were designated as *Asprishya Sudra*, 'those whose touch is so impure as to pollute even the Ganges water' (as quoted in Ibid.: 4).

However, the concept of 'untouchability' originated in the writings of the local reformers. The social and religious reform movements that were initiated by Western-educated Indians, members of the newly emergent middle class, during the second half of the nineteenth century viewed the exclusion and marginalization of 'low' castes as an important area for reform of Hindu society. Though they all came from the upper crust of the Indian society, they approached the question of caste from their nascent democratic imagination. Charsley says that one of the first statements on the subject of untouchability was made by

G.K. Gokhale, in a resolution he moved in a confer-
ence of social reformers at Dharwar in 1903. It is worth
quoting from the statement: 'We may touch a cat, we
may touch a dog... but the touch of these human
beings is pollution. And so complete is now the mental
degradation of these people that they themselves see
nothing in such treatment to resent...' (as quoted in
Ibid.: 6).

Though the upper-caste reformers were talking
about untouchability and pollution, the popular category through which they identified 'these people'
was the 'Depressed Classes'. The term had been in
use since the 1870s. By the early twentieth century
several bodies were set up by the reformers in different parts of India focusing on the question of welfare
of the 'Depressed Classes'. However, a section among
them argued that the word 'depressed' did not con-
vey the specific form of disability experienced by
those 'inflicted' by pollution. The Maharaja of Baroda,
Sayaji Rao Gaekwad III, wrote in 1909 in *The Indian
Review* that 'untouchableness' was 'additional to more
widely shared difficulties such as poverty and illiteracy'.
He also criticized the term 'depressed classes' for being
'too elastic' to include even those from the Brahmin

caste, who did not experience 'pollution'. The 'specially disadvantaged therefore needed another title: untouchable', he proposed (Ibid.: 7). Gradually the term took off and by the 1920s it was also being used by the colonial rulers in their administrative reports. Though Gandhi too used the term untouchability in some of his initial writings, he eventually opted for the term Harijan (God's people), coined in the previous century by a Brahmin Gujarati saint poet Narsinh Mehta.

The experience or reality of untouchability had indeed been a fact of life. However, its construction and acceptance by the colonial state and the nationalist politics completely changed the discourse on caste and it has had far-reaching implications for the way caste came to be understood, and for the way the state was to engage with it. This conceptual shift continues to play a critical role in contemporary India. Simon Charsley classifies the implications of this conceptual shift into five different categories. First of all it helped establish an 'all- India standard', a classificatory system that could be used everywhere. A second related implication of focusing on 'untouchables' was that it helped in 'subsuming different castes' within one title, 'a spurious social definiteness and homogeneity' (Rudolph and Rudolph 1967: 134). Despite empirical divergences and differences in structures of caste hierarchy across regions and communities of India, the practice of untouchability was common. The term 'untouchables', as Charsley puts it, 'masks local heterogeneity as well as setting up a uniformity more apparent than real between areas. It simplifies the problem of understanding Indian society at the cost of obscuring the need to come to terms with one of its major and analytically important characteristics: diversity' (1996: 11).

The third important implication of this conceptual move was that it 'dichotomized' caste and society into two categories, the touchables and untouchables. Though different people used different categories, the discourse was mostly in dichotomous terms. Different sets of categories that became popular included 'caste: outcastes' or its Sanskrit version *Savarna: Avarna*; Caste Hindu: Untouchable; high–caste: low–caste.

Fourth, the idea of untouchability automatically 'prioritized pollution-related exclusion' as the most distinctive/important feature of the caste system. Though it was a negative and an undesirable feature of the caste system and Indian society, it provided an easy point of focus. The focus on pollution-related exclusion also meant that 'it was not a problem of poverty as such, or powerlessness deriving from dependence on those who owned the land in an agrarian society, but a matter of belief and related behaviour' (Ibid.: 12). Thus, the challenge for reformers like Gandhi was to mobilize popular opinion for changing mental dispositions towards the untouchables and uplifting them socially, which effectively translated into bringing them into the Hindu fold by allowing them to enter Hindu temples. Finally, the focus on untouchability represented those identified as being below the line of pollution as 'victims only'. This mode of representation also stigmatized them and constructed their identities only in negative terms. While in reality, Charsley argues, 'every caste, whether it has been labelled 'untouchable' or not, has its positive identity' (Ibid.: 12), a point we discuss in greater detail later in this chapter.

From Untouchables to Scheduled Castes

Perhaps the most far-reaching implication of the growing use of the categories of 'depressed classes' and untouchables/untouchability during the early years of the twentieth century was its official recognition in the Government of India Act of 1935. It initiated the process of listing of certain caste communities in an official Schedule, which was to be used for identifying social groups needing special attention of the colonial state. 'The invention of Scheduled Caste' (Galanter 1984: 121–30) as an officially recognized category for listing deprived communities was also closely tied to the idea of untouchability.

Interestingly, those who framed the Act of 1935 were not easily convinced that untouchability existed in the same form everywhere in India. There were significant differences between the south and the north. The ideas of pollution and untouchability were not as significant in some parts of the north as they were in Madras (Chennai), Bombay (Mumbai), and the Central Provinces. Thus, though untouchability was a critical criterion, it alone did not determine inclusion of a group. 'Criteria for inclusion had to be multiple, and concerned with disadvantage more generally' (Ibid.: 14). Thus, the lists of communities to be categorized as SCs were prepared state-wise and they differed 'both in terms of names included and in the bases for their inclusion'. They were published as Schedules attached to the Act, hence 'Scheduled Castes', and the people concerned came to be popularly designated as 'SCs' (Ibid.: 14). One of the obvious implications of this is that the popular perception which equates SCs with ex-untouchables is not entirely correct. Notwithstanding the procedural niceties, the category of SC only reinforced what the idea of the 'line-of-pollution' or untouchability had done to the popular understanding and imaginings of caste.

The moral discourse of reforms in relation to untouchability also translated into a set of legislations, penal acts to remedy and remove its practice. The first of these legislations was passed in the present-day state of Kerala, The Travancore-Cochin Removal of Disabilities Act, 1825. In 1938 the Madras legislature passed a similar Act, followed by Baroda and Mysore in 1939 and 1943, respectively. Untouchability was finally abolished by the Constitution of independent India in 1950 under Article 17 and its practice was made an offence. As the Act states:

'Untouchability' is abolished and its practice in any form is forbidden. The enforcement of any disability arising out of 'Untouchability' shall be an offence punishable in accordance with law.

Over the years, the Government of India enacted a few more legislations to protect the SCs from violence of different kinds. These include the Untouchability Offence Act in 1955; Protection of Civil Rights Act in 1976; and Scheduled Castes and Scheduled Tribes Prevention of Atrocities Act in 1989.

The Constitution of independent India also incorporated the idea and list of SCs from the 1935 Act and, over the years, expanded it. The Government of India also expanded on the affirmative action provisions for the welfare and development of SCs, a subject discussed in the next chapter. As per the Census of 2001, the total SC population in India was 166,635,700, making for 16.2 per cent of the total population of the country. The northern state of Uttar Pradesh had the largest SC population (35,148,377), followed by West Bengal (18,452,555) and Bihar (13,048,608). In proportional terms, Punjab was at the top with 28.85 per cent of its population being SCs. Though caste and untouchability are often treated as pan-Indian realities, there are several states in India where in proportional or absolute terms the presence of SCs is very low or negligible. These are the states in the north-east of India (except Assam) where the SC population is less than 1 per cent and Goa where less than 2 per cent of the population is listed as SC. Each of the Indian states has its own list of SCs. A total of 1,231 communities are currently listed as SCs in the entire country.

Sociology of Untouchability

The formal or legal abolition of the practice of untouchability did not mean the end of the dualistic conceptions of caste, sociologically or ontologically. As mentioned in the previous chapters and at the beginning of this chapter, despite their critical role in constructing theories of caste and inventing new categories of difference and aggregation, the idea of pollution and hierarchy are not simply mental constructs that emerge with the introduction of new categories of enumeration. Rural settlements in different parts of the subcontinent were designed in a manner that those from the untouchable caste communities lived away from the main settlements, even when their services were required by the village community. Given their segregation from the village community and their employment in 'low-value' jobs, they lived in miserable and humiliating social conditions.

However, the classical sociological and anthropological writings on the subject rarely looked at them from such a perspective. They were often seen to be a part of the system, functionally and ideologically integrated in the structural framework of caste. As discussed in Chapter 1, Brahmins and the Untouchables were seen as the two necessary and mutually oppositional elements of the caste system. The ideological conformity across caste groups, from top to bottom, ensured its reproduction. This assumption has, however, been a major source of contention among the students of caste. Our discussion in Chapter 2 clearly shows that such a contention was often contested from the middle. The ritual and material superiority of Brahmins in relation to the middle-level dominant castes as constructed from the scriptural sources was often contradicted by the empirical studies of the village society. The ritual superiority of a Brahmin needed to be supplemented by his material strength for it to be ideologically realized. In regions where Brahmins had no material wealth, their position carried little honour.

Even the 'ritual orders' and their meanings, as shown by G.G. Raheja varied across regions. In other words, there were different ideological systems governing the social ordering of caste in different regions of the subcontinent.

The sociological and social anthropological studies focusing on untouchability and the communities located below the line of pollution also present diverse pictures on the ideological order of caste.

However, notwithstanding the fact of diversity, we must also underline the point that though its intensity and forms varied, untouchability was practised almost everywhere in India, even in regions where being a Brahmin did not carry much prestige. The idea of pollution has also been strategically and politically useful to different actors in different ways. While it helped the colonial rulers in making sense of the caste system in the midst of the wide-ranging diversities that they encountered, particularly when they started carrying out decadal census, for the religious reformists and nationalists, it was a useful point for coming together. It helped them establish, albeit negatively, that India did have a unified tradition, a common history and a common value-frame. This notion of unity helped those trying to argue in favour of the idea of a unified Hindu religion and a unified Indian civilization. Given that orientalists had conceptualized caste as a Hindu institution, the practice and presence of untouchability could easily be cited as evidence of the widespread prevalence of the Hindu cultural influence in the subcontinent.

Within the sociological and social anthropological scholarship, the idea of untouchability has been a subject of controversy and contention. For the classical Dumontian sociology, caste was a unified system based on a religious ideology, which produced a consensus on the values of purity and impurity across the hierarchical social order. Those located at the bottom of the caste hierarchy were as much involved and committed to the reproduction of the order of purity and pollution as those at the top. Even when they were individually unhappy about their position in the system, or with the system, they accepted it. The only available option for exiting the system was renunciation (*sanyas*), by leaving community and the normal 'worldly' life.

In an influential book published in 1979, Michael Moffat, nearly confirmed this thesis on the basis of his ethnographic work *An Untouchable Community of South India.* The untouchables of his village were well-integrated into the caste system and functionally complemented it:

> Untouchables possess and act upon a thickly textured culture whose fundamental definition and values are identical to those of a more global Indian village culture. The 'view from the bottom' is based on the same principles and evaluations as 'the view from the middle' or 'the view from the top'. The cultural system of Indian Untouchables does not distinctly question or revalue the dominant social order. Rather, it continuously recreates among Untouchables the microcosm of the larger system. (1979: 3)

Moffat goes a step further and argues that not only do the untouchables live in *consensus* with the Hindu caste system and *complement* it ritually and ideologically, they also *replicate* it among themselves. He identified five different caste groups occupying different positions in the hierarchy of castes among the untouchables in the Tamil Nadu village he studied. The 'replicatory order was constructed in the same cultural code that marked highness and lowness, purity and impurity, super-ordination and subordination, among the higher castes. It thus implies ... a deep cultural consensus on the cognitive and evaluative assumptions of the system as a whole' (Ibid.: 98).

Moffat's work and his arguments are significant contributions to the study of caste as they help us recognize the limitations and problems of the dualistic mode of thinking about caste. However, many scholars have questioned its empirical validity. No serious scholar of caste would perhaps disagree with Moffat about the fact that the untouchables are themselves internally divided among sub-groups and castes and that these groups have an internal structure of hierarchy. However, it is hard to concede that everyone was equally in agreement with the ideological frame of caste. In other words, his notions of 'consensus, complementarily and replication' as the working parameters of caste system appear like an overstatement.

In a paper published in 1974, Joan Mencher tried to construct an account of the caste system by turning it upside down, from the viewpoint of those located at the bottom of the caste hierarchy. 'From the point of view of the people at the lowest end of the scale, caste has functioned, and continues to function as a very effective system of economic exploitation' (Mencher 1974: 469). She also questions 'the high-caste point of view ... that low-caste people have always accepted their position ... It is quite clear that it was the superior economic and political power of the upper castes that kept the lower ones suppressed' (Ibid.: 471). More importantly perhaps, she questions the popular assumption and understanding of caste that equates caste with occupational differentiation and presents each caste as being engaged in a particular occupation, the calling of their caste. With the exception of a few small castes, in most cases, 'only a small proportion' of the caste members actually do the work that is identified with the caste, such as leatherwork and Chamars, 'and only a small proportion of their time has traditionally been spent on in'. In most of rural India, a large majority of the untouchables was part of the local agrarian economy and worked as agricultural labourers. The function of the caste system was to keep them divided.

Though Mencher too studied the rural setting of Tamil Nadu, her ethnography does not support the point made by Moffat about consensus on the core

values of the system across castes. As she narrates from
her fieldwork:

> When questioned about various caste practices, some
> Harijans at first say things like 'It is their right. We are
> untouchables'. But, when pressed, they offer explana-
> tions like 'they own all the land' or 'even the poor
> Naickers have the support of the rich ones, none of us
> has much land', or as one girl put, 'We can't ask them
> to do some work for us. No! Instead of that those
> people only take work out of us, so naturally they
> are supposed to be higher than we are … if we made
> any complaint, they would simply refuse to allow us
> to work on their land; and then what to do, we will
> simply starve. (Ibid.: 476)

A similar point is also made by Dipankar Gupta
who too questions the assumption that everyone in
the caste system subscribed to the Brahmin's view of
caste. Every other caste located below the so-called
pollution line has a tale to tell about its origins that
explains the caste divisions in a variety of ways:

> Not always is the occupation aspect uppermost
> in these tales of genesis. But when in the tales of
> origin of the so-called lower castes the occupational

aspect is stressed ... then the occupation is not seen as a particularly degrading one.... In occupational evaluations, and in other aspects too, individual caste ideologies differ markedly from the Brahmanical versions. (Gupta 1984: 2003)

The so-called low castes also contested the reasons given by those above them for their degradation: 'The truth is that no caste, howsoever lowly placed it may be, accepts the reasons for its degradation. Harijans, of whatever jati, do not accept the upper-caste view that their bodies are made of impure substance' (Gupta 2000: 1).

While the structure of hierarchy is questioned, the ideas of hierarchy and pollution are not, argues Gupta, '... while no caste is willing to concede that its own members are defiling, they readily allege that there are other castes that are indeed polluting. This tendency holds even among the so-called untouchable castes ...' (Ibid.: 1–2).

The origin myths of untouchable communities collected by Robert Deliège from different parts of the country also substantiate the point made by Gupta. Though the 'origin myths' popular with untouchable communities differ in their format and emphasis, none of them subscribes to the Brahmanical mythology of the origin of the caste system as presented in *Manusmriti*. Even when these origin-myths accept the hierarchical reality of caste as given, 'as a matter of fact', untouchables do not attribute their low status to something being 'inherently bad about them'. Interestingly, all across India, the untouchable communities explain their lowly status in terms of 'a misunderstanding', 'a trick', 'a pun', or 'crookedness' of others (Deliège 1993: 536). The origin-myths popular among untouchables also tended to present them as being originally superior to the Brahmin, but having lost their position for one or the other reason. One of the myths popular among the Paraiyars of Tamil Nadu, presented by Deliège is worth quoting here:

> In the beginning, there were two brothers who were poor. Then they went together to pray to God. God asked them to remove the carcass of a dead cow. The elder brother answered: '*Eenthambipappan*' (My younger brother will do it) but understood: '*Eenthambipaappan*' (My younger brother is a Brahmin); since that very day, the younger brother became Brahman (paappaan) and the elder brother became a

Paraiyar. All castes originate from these two brothers.
(Ibid.: 536)

Similarly, another anthropologist reported from
Uttar Pradesh that the sweepers of Khalapur did not
believe that their current low status was in any way a
punishment for the deeds of past lives. Instead, they saw
it in terms of 'a terrible historical accident' (Kolenda
cited in Ibid.: 538). Similarly, Berreman reported from
his fieldwork that none of his informants said that he
'was a scoundrel in a previous life and now he was getting his just deserts' (Berreman 1963: 223). He also did
not find his respondents fatalistic. No one explained
their 'low' status by saying that they 'had always done
defiling work. This is what they were created to do and
therefore they were untouchables' (Ibid.: 223, single
quotes in original).

Even when the untouchables themselves subscribed
to the idea of hierarchy and practised it in relation to
themselves, within the communities below the pollution line, they had no reverence for the Brahmin.
The untouchables in south India viewed Brahmins
as 'greedy', 'lazy', 'ridiculous', and 'avaricious'. In contrast, they see themselves as the 'auspicious providers
of agricultural bounty', 'generous', and 'hardwork-

91

ing' (Deliège 1993: 541; Lynch 1969; Djurfeldt and Lindberg 1975: 219). Deliège cites an interesting quote from Kathleen Gough's ethnography of the untouchables of Tanjore district (Tamil Nadu):

> One day, sitting in the Adi-Dravida Street, I tackled a group of older Pallars...I asked them where they thought the soul went after death...The groups collapsed in merriment...Wiping his eyes the old man replied, 'Mother, we don't know! Do you know? Have you been there?' I said 'No, but Brahmins say that if people do their duty well in this life, their souls will be born next time in a higher caste'. 'Brahmins say!' scoffed another elder. 'Brahmins say anything. Their heads go round and round!' (as quoted in Deliège 1993: 533–4)

An important implication of these writings is that even though the idea of hierarchy is central to caste, on ground there is no single hierarchy, as has been suggested by scholars like Dumont. Once we recognize the presence of multiple hierarchies, caste no longer remains a completely closed system. It opens up the possibilities of contestations and negotiations, which indeed has been the fact in history.

Untouchability Today

Whatever might have been the case in the past, there would be very few among the ex-untouchables today who would regard themselves as impure or justify their low status on grounds of their misconduct in some previous life, a 'fact of nature' (Charsley and Karanth 1998). The two most important things that have happened in relation to the practice of untouchability are: (a) its legal de-recognition and (b) a near-complete change in the consciousness of those at the receiving end of the hierarchical system. The ex-untouchable communities have almost everywhere become much more assertive about their human and political rights (Mendelsohn and Vicziany 2000: 1). Today they 'all aspire to more comfortable material circumstances; all demand more dignity' (Deliège 1999: 1).

The processes of economic development, urbanization, and political change have also introduced new spheres of social interaction, which were designed to be caste-free or open to all. For example, the introduction of a public transport system, state-funded primary and higher education, healthcare, and many other modern-day services to rural areas were to be provided to all, irrespective of caste and creed. Some of these modern provisions, such as the tap water, were to also become an alternative to the traditionally available services, such as the community well. Even though the element of caste crept into these provisions as well, its presence was lesser. For example, a survey conducted by I.P. Desai in Gujarat in the early 1970s reported that though the practice of untouchability was quite prevalent in rural areas, its practice was minimal in bus travel, in post offices, and in schools. However, its practice in the 'private' sphere was much more. In as many as 90 per cent of the villages, untouchables were not allowed entry into the upper-caste houses. Untouchability was also practised widely in the seating arrangement in the village panchayats in Gujarat.

More than twenty-five years after the Gujarat survey of I.P. Desai, an all-India survey of rural settlements across eleven states of India carried out during 2001–2 found that though the ground reality of caste had indeed been changing, the practice of untouchability had not completely ended. More importantly, perhaps, there is no radical alleviation in the social and economic conditions of a large majority of untouchables. The survey reported: '... untouchability is not only present all over rural India, but it has survived by adapting to new socioeconomic realities and taking on new and insidious forms ... Untouchability continues to be an important component of the experience of being Dalit in contemporary India, especially the countryside ...' (Shah et al. 2006: 15–16).

Though the association of caste with occupation has over the years become much weaker with almost all castes diversifying into different occupations, the occupations identified with the ex-untouchables are still carried out almost exclusively by them. For example, even though a very small proportion of all those who are identified with the occupation of scavenging earn their livelihood through their traditional occupation, almost all scavengers are from the caste communities identified with the occupation. Apart from the low social status that these occupations carry in the Indian society, they are also low-paying and often high-risk occupations.

A study that collected data from more than 500 villages reported that almost everywhere the rural settlements are divided on caste lines, particularly so in relation to the ex-untouchables. Almost everywhere they live away from the main settlement and the dominant/upper castes continue to impose restrictions on their visit to the main village. In more than 48 per cent of the studied villages, the ex-untouchable communities were not allowed access to the common water source of the village. Similarly, in around one-third of the villages, the local teashops and restaurants used separate utensils for customers from ex-untouchable communities. More than 70 per cent of the villages imposed restrictions on inter-dining with the ex-untouchables and they were also not allowed entry into upper-caste houses. In more than 60 per cent of the villages, they were not allowed entry into temples. In around one-fourth of the villages, they had no choice but to 'stand up' in the presence of an upper-caste person (Ibid.). While the practice of untouchability had indeed declined in some parts of India and in some spheres of social life, the incidence of its continuity is also quite significant.

From Untouchability to Atrocities

An important implication of the gradual process of economic development and social change has been the disintegration of the traditional system of caste-based hierarchies and weakening of the ideological apparatus supporting the caste system. Decline in the practice of untouchability has been an obvious implication of this process of change. However, notwithstanding all these changes, the inequalities have persisted. The dominant caste communities resist democratization of social relations and do not take kindly to the growing self-assertion and desire for citizenship status among the ex-untouchables. Thus, even though the older forms of untouchability have receded, atrocities committed on Dalits by the local dominant castes have persisted, and in some cases, become more brutal (Mendelsohn and Vicziany 2000; Béteille 2000; Shah 2001). Even when the old caste-ties do not make any economic sense, and the ex-untouchables no longer depend on the caste-based economy, the locally dominant caste insists on their observing caste boundaries. Any assertion by the historically marginalized is seen as transgression and the reaction of the dominant caste is invariably violent.

One of the most popular methods of dealing with Dalit assertion and 'teaching them a lesson' has been the social boycott of the entire ex-untouchable community by the dominant castes in the village. The ex-untouchables in rural India have also been landless and thus dependent on the dominant caste communities for their economic sustenance. Social boycott means no employment within the village. They are also prohibited from using the village commons, which has traditionally been used by the poor for collecting fodder and firewood. They may even face hardships in sending children to the local schools. If the boycott continues for a long time, it has far-reaching negative consequences for the subordinate communities. Such boycotts have been reported from different parts of the country and in some cases they can continue for over a year.

Apart from collective social boycott, the ex-untouchables also encounter direct violence, often directed against the entire community including those who do not participate in Dalit assertion movements, 'extravagant revenge' (Mendelsohn and Vicziany 2000; Gorringe 2005). Reports of such violence have increased over the years. One of the first cases of large-scale violence against the Dalits was reported in December 1968 from a place called Kilvenmani located in the Thanjavur district of Tamil Nadu where forty-two Dalits were burnt to death because they had decided to organize themselves and protest against the low wages. They were all locked up in a hut and set on fire. In a similar incident in the year 1977, in the village of Dharampura in Bihar, the landowners killed four 'untouchable' sharecroppers because they were unwilling to give up their legal claim over the land they had been cultivating for decades. Dalits are not always attacked for economic reasons. While 'violence in some cases has been overtly economic in origin, there have been others where violence has been the result of "Untouchable" challenges to the traditional ritual norms' (Joshi 1982: 676).

In a place called Karamchedu in Andhra Pradesh seven Dalits were killed by the dominant Kammas in 1985 because the Dalits protested against the upper castes washing their cattle in the village tank from where the Dalits obtained their drinking water. In another incident in 1991, in the state of Andhra Pradesh, nine Dalits were killed by the local landlords for some trivial reason. In 2006, in a place called Khairlanji in Maharashtra the entire family of a Dalit farmer was brutally murdered by a group of dominant caste men because he had complained to the local police against them for harassing and physically assaulting him (Mohanty 2007).

Apart from these 'spectacular' cases, the ex-untouchables also experience everyday violence and humiliation of various kinds, ranging from physical beating of individuals to rape, murder, and mental torture of various kinds. Young Dalit men have also been victims of 'honour-killings' when they married a woman from the dominant caste. A large number of caste-related crimes continue to be reported against Dalits (see Table 1). These are all reported crimes and given the nature of the social system in India, not all cases of crimes get registered with the police. The continued existence of the practice of untouchability, even though to a lesser degree, and rather frequent reports of atrocities against Dalits, clearly point to the persistence of their marginal position in the larger economy and social structure of the Indian society.

The most frequently cited reason for incidents of violence against the ex-untouchables is their growing assertion, while they are still dependent on traditionally dominant communities.

TABLE 1 Comparative Incidence of Crime against Scheduled Castes

S.no.	Crime head	2001	2012	2003	2004	2005	% Variation in 2005 over 2004
1.	Murder	763	739	581	654	669	2.3
2.	Rape	1,316	1,331	1,089	1,157	1,172	1.3
3.	Kidnapping and abduction	400	319	232	253	258	2.0
4.	Dacoity	41	29	24	26	26	0.0
5.	Robbery	133	105	70	72	80	11.1
6.	Arson	354	322	204	211	210	−0.5
7.	Hurt	4,547	4,491	3,969	3,824	3,847	0.6
8.	Protection of Civil Rights Act	633	1,018	634	364	291	−20.0
9.	SC/ST (Prevention of Atrocities) Act	13,113	10,770	8,048	8,891	8,497	−4.4
10.	Others	12,201	14,383	114,351	11,435	11,077	−3.1
	Total	33,501	33,507	26,252	26,887	26,127	−2.8

Source: Crime in India 2005, National Crime Records Bureau, Ministry of Home Affairs, as in *Eleventh Five Year Plan*, Volume 1, Planning Commission. Available at http://planningcommission.nic.in/plans/planrel/fiveyr/11th/11_v1/11th_vol1.pdf (p. 103), accessed on 20 October 2009.

The ex-untouchables' assertion for dignity has a long and dynamic history and reflects the larger process of change taking place in the Indian society and in the social order of caste. We focus on the changing nature of social hierarchies of caste in the next chapter.

4

Contesting Caste

The institution of caste is almost universally viewed as a conservative mode of social organization. As we have seen in the first chapter, the classical sociological and social anthropological literature equated caste with traditional social life, a typical example of a closed system of social stratification. Even among the traditional institutions, caste is viewed as most rigid, never-changing, and encompassing almost every aspect of the Hindu social life. As this popular understanding of Indian society goes, caste originated in the ancient past. Along with its social universe, the Indian village, it survived all kinds of political upheavals. This understanding of caste and the Indian society was a product of European encounters with the Indian civilization during the nineteenth century. In the 'mainstream' social science literature, one of the most influential statements of this perspective on the subject is by Karl Marx. Presenting his views on the social organization of the Indian village and the caste system, Marx wrote: '... these little communities were contaminated by distinctions of caste and by slavery, that they subjugated man to external circumstances instead of elevating man, the sovereign of circumstances, that they transformed a self-developing social state into never-changing natural destiny ...' (1853).

In this context, also underlining the historic significance of the British colonial rule in transforming the Indian society, Marx goes on to say, '... whatever may have been the crimes of England she was the unconscious tool of history in bringing about ... revolution' (Ibid.).

Marx was certainly not the only one who viewed caste as the source of India's presumed social and economic 'stagnation'. He was articulating what had become the common-sense understanding of the Indian society in Western Europe during the nineteenth century. Caste was seen as being critical in slowing down, or even inhibiting, the process of change because it made Indians accept their situation even if it was exploitative and depressing, as part of their destiny, their karma. Extending this thesis to the agrarian history, the famous historian of contemporary India, Barrington Moore Jr., attributed the relative passivity of Indian peasants during the colonial and pre-colonial period to the 'peculiar structure of peasant society, organized through caste system' (1966: 315).

In the mainstream social sciences, such as economics, sociology and political science, this notion of Indian society is quite explicit in the ways in which 'cultural pre-conditions' of modernization and development were theorized in the post-Second World War period. They all underlined the need to do away with the traditional institutions like caste if India had to become a 'modern' and democratic society, like countries of the West (see, for example, Inkeles and Smith 1974).

This 'Western' view of caste was also internalized by 'modern Indians'. For example, Jawaharlal Nehru, India's first Prime Minister, a representative modern Indian, described 'the caste system and much that goes with it' as 'wholly incompatible, reactionary, restrictive, and barriers to progress' (Nehru 1946: 257). For an average middle-class modern Indian of the 1950s and 1960s, 'caste was among the few traditional institutions that were presented as all bad, as "social evils" without any redeeming features' (Deshpande 2003: 1998). Thus, notwithstanding Gandhi's defence of the Indian village and it social organization based on a division of labour on caste lines, the idea of caste did not find any defenders in the post-independence Indian state. Even though the post-independence Indian state did not take any radical measures to 'annihilate caste', it did initiate measures to alleviate the disparities and exclusions that caste presumably produced. It did so through legal, administrative, and development measures. Thanks to these measures, the institution of caste has indeed experienced a set of changes over the last century or so.

However, it is not only during the last century that the institution of caste has seen changes. As I have tried to argue in the previous chapters, caste has never been static. Like any other social institution, caste too has been a fluid structure, empirically as well as conceptually. It is certainly not true that the caste system had remained intact for centuries and it began to change only in the nineteenth and twentieth century under the British colonial rule. The social organization of caste often changed with the changing political order.

Similarly, historians have shown that the economy of the so-called Indian village was never stagnant, and as the economic orders changed, caste relations also underwent alterations (see, for example, Neale 1962; Habib 1963). This chapter provides a brief introduction to the forces that have been working against the idea of caste hierarchy, from below and from above. Much before the British introduced Western education and modern technology, there had been several instances in history when caste was challenged. These contestations also produced profound changes in the social relations at the regional level and beyond.

Initiatives from Below

A large volume of historical and anthropological research shows that notwithstanding the claims of ideological consensus, those located at the lower end of the hierarchy did not always accept their position in the caste system as a natural consequence of their past karma. They often attributed it to the manipulations and deceitful action of others. In other words, Sanskritization was not the only mode through which groups in the social order would have changed their position in the caste hierarchy. Political and material struggles would have also played their role. Similarly, changing economic and demographic realities would have also influenced the social order of caste.

Interestingly, the protest movements and contestation of caste invariably appeared in religious forms. Perhaps the first major movement against the caste system was the rise of Buddhism in ancient times. Gautam Buddha, the founder of Buddhism, underlined the unity of humankind. He professed that all human beings, irrespective of caste and creed, have a common predicament of life and face *dukha* (suffering). Buddha proposed an eightfold path to salvation. He also 'rejuvenated and reorganized the prevailing social and religious system by denouncing the ritual sacrifice and priesthood of Brahmins and laid stress on the individual's own efforts to achieve nirvana' (salvation) (Keer cited in Ghuman 2011: 12–13). Contrary to the Brahmanism of his time, 'the Buddha taught the essential equality of the possibilities of liberation available to all' (Klostermaier cited in Ibid.: 13). The Buddhist ideology not only acquired popularity but it also became a state religion in ancient India under rulers like Ashoka. It was from the Indian soil that Buddhism travelled to different parts of Asia. However, for various historical reasons, its influence declined in India after being an important faith in the region for several centuries.

The order of caste and the supremacy of the Brahmin were challenged again during the so-called medieval times by the saint poets like Kabir, Ravidas, and Nanak among many others. Some of these saints, such as Ravidas and Kabir (Lele 1981; Lorenzen 1987), are believed to have themselves come from communities located close to the bottom of the traditional caste hierarchy. Quite like the Buddha, they too criticized Brahmanical orthodoxy and advocated universal values of equality and dignity. God, they advocated, did not create distinctions of caste. Neither did He like the ritualism advocated by the Brahmins. Some of their hymns directly attack Brahmins and Brahmanical ideology. The English translation of one of the hymns by Kabir is quite explicit about this:

> Pandit, look in your heart for knowledge
> Tell me where untouchability
> Came from, since you believe in it.
> We eat by touching,
> we wash by touching, from a touch

The world was born.
So who's untouched? Asks Kabir
Only he
Who has no taint of Maya.
And
It's all one skin and bone
One piss and shit
One blood, one meat
From one drop, a universe.
Who's Brahmin? Who's Shudra? (as in Ghuman
2011: 14)

Similarly, Ravidas, who too was born in a 'low'-caste Chamar family near the town of Banaras in present-day Uttar Pradesh, constructed a notion of Utopia where everyone was treated equally and fairly. His hymn 'Begumpura', imagines of a city without sorrows, 'where there will be no distress, no tax, no restriction from going and coming, no fear'. Its English translation goes like this:

The regal realm with the sorrow-less name:
they call it Begumpura,
a place with no pain,
No taxes or cares,
nor own property there,

no wrongdoing, worry, terror or torture.
Oh my brother,
I have come to take it as my own,
my distant home,
where everything is right.
That imperial kingdom is rich and secure,
where none are third or second—all are one;
Its food and drink are famous,
and those who live there
dwell in satisfaction and in wealth.
They do this or that,
they walk where they wish,
they stroll through fabled places unchallenged.
Oh, says Ravidas, a tanner now set free,
those who walk beside me are my friends.

Another poet from this tradition, Karma Mela, a Mahar Dalit and son of the fourteenth-century saint poet Choka Mela of Maharashtra, articulated his angst against caste in even stronger words:

You made us impure
I don't know why Lord
We've eaten leftovers all our life
Doesn't that trouble you
Our house stocked with rice and yogurt

How do you refuse it
Chokha's Karma Mela asks
Why did you give me birth?
(as in Mendelsohn and Vicziany 2000: 24)

The saint poets like Ravidas and Kabir attracted a large following. An evidence of the influence of their writings is the fact that the Sikh Gurus included their writings in the holy book they were compiling during the sixteenth and seventeenth centuries. During the 1970s and 1980s, the activists began to reinvent some of these writings and symbolisms to inspire many in the contemporary Dalit movements (see Jodhka 2009; Omvedt 2008).

Modern-day Reformist Movements

Religious reform movements initiated by the newly emergent middle classes during the British colonial period also raised questions of reforming Hindu family life and the caste system. Though their primary impetus to reform Hinduism generally came from the perceived threat of conversion of the 'low' castes to Christianity, and their own anxiety of trying to live up to the Western standards of 'civilized cultures', these movements have had far-reaching implications on the institution and practice of caste, though not always in a positive vein for the marginalized in the caste system. One of the most important and influential movements in this category was the 'neo-Vedantic' Arya Samaj movement.

With the objective of strengthening Hinduism and stopping conversions of 'low' castes to other religious systems, the Arya Samajis criticized some of the prevailing practices among the Hindus, which often also included the practice of untouchability. Its founder, Swami Dayananda, advocated going back to the ancient Vedic religion wherein untouchables were presumably a part of Hindu religion. He attacked Brahmanical hegemony in religious affairs and emphasized the need for spreading modern education among the Hindus. He advocated inclusion of the lower castes into the Hindu society through a process of religious purification, the *Shuddhi*. If untouchability emanated from ritual impurity, it could also be removed through religious rituals, enabling untouchables to become touchable. This movement became quite popular in Punjab and has been well-documented by scholars (Dua 1970; Sharma 1985; 1987; Pimpley and Sharma 1985).

What did the shuddhi movement do for the untouchables and what difference did it make to their status, within the Hindu society and beyond? Did it work towards getting them accepted as equals in the Hindu religion?

Looking at Punjab, Pimpley and Sharma (1985) found that the movement did not really make any significant difference to the untouchables though it helped the Punjabi Hindu elite in consolidating their position in the region. 'The Punjabi Hindu elite succeeded, in large measure, to retain the untouchable castes in the Hindu fold thereby increasing their political strength'. As far as the untouchables were concerned, they found that a majority of those who went through the shuddhi ceremony 'still suffered from poverty and the stigma of untouchability. Their educational levels were very low. Occupationally they were engaged in agricultural labour or in low-prestige jobs. Their geographical segregation suggested minimum level of social interaction with other castes. Probably, even after their shuddhi, they did not gain anything except for a symbolic right of reading the Vedas and putting on the sacred thread' (Ibid.: 98).

More importantly, perhaps, despite their criticism of the Brahmanical orthodoxy within Hinduism, the strategy of Arya Samaj for elevating the status of the untouchables was worked out within the framework of purity and impurity. Though they condemned the practice of untouchability, they did not reject the concept of varna. The very notion of shuddhi involved the affirmation of the idea of ritual purity as being the criterion for status enhancement.

This was also the case with some other reform movements of the times. Gooptu, for example, shows in her work on the *Adi*-Hindu movement in Uttar Pradesh that quite like the Arya Samajis in Punjab, its leaders did not directly attack the caste system, or criticize Hindu religion (Gooptu 2001). Such Adi movements came up in other parts of the subcontinent as well (see Shah 1975; 2004). The primary objective of these movements was perhaps to make sure that untouchables remained within Hinduism and did not convert to Christianity or Islam. This had become quite important in the context where demographic numbers had begun to acquire political meanings with the rise of nationalist sentiments on religious lines.

Alternative or Radical Movements

Historical trajectories of the alternative or radical 'low'-caste movements are quite similar to that of the reform movements. They also emerged during the British colonial period. In fact, some of them emerged out of, or in response to the Hindu reform movements. Perhaps the most well known in this category of social movements were the non-Brahmin movements in the south of India (Pandian 1996) and Maharashtra (Omvedt 1976). These movements were initiated mostly by those who belonged to what were known as the 'backward castes', which did not always include the untouchables. However, the 'backward caste' movements did criticize the caste hierarchy and Brahmanical cultural and social systems. By doing so, they created a space for the emergence of Dalit movements. No wonder later-day radical and autonomous Dalit movements mostly emerged in regions where non-Brahmin movements had been strong.

Initiated by members of the rich and upwardly mobile rural/agrarian castes (Rao 1979; Irschick 1969) in the southern state of Tamil Nadu, the non-Brahmin movements questioned the supremacy of Brahmins in all spheres of life. Later, a section of the movement also critiqued Hinduism and religion in general. Some of their leaders openly advocated atheism. It was in Maharashtra that backward caste movements first paved the way for the Dalit movements (Omvedt 1976), culminating in conversion to Buddhism by a section of Maharashtra Dalits in 1956 under the leadership of B.R. Ambedkar (Wilkinson and Thomas 1972; Zelliot 1977; Omvedt 1976; 1994; Joshi 1986; Beltz 2005). This movement mobilized the Mahar Dalits of Maharashtra and has come to be known as the neo-Buddhist movement. This movement has played a critical role in shaping the contemporary Dalit identity and therefore needs to be discussed in some detail.

According to the Colonial Census of 1931, Mahars were the most numerous of the untouchable castes of Maharashtra and accounted for about 11 per cent of the total population of the colonial province (total population of all the untouchable communities put together was 16.47 per cent). As a caste group, their size was second only to that of the dominant caste of the Marathas (who were 20.2 per cent). They were counted among the untouchables but, as pointed out by Jaffrelot (2004: 20), in terms of the local status hierarchy, Mahars were the first among the last.

B.R. Ambedkar was born in a Mahar family that had greatly benefited from recruitment in the colonial army. Having grown up in a cantonment area, Ambedkar escaped much of the prejudice and violence of the caste system that his fellow Mahars experienced in a typical rural setting of Maharashtra. However, he could not escape this reality for very long. Fighting against caste-based prejudice and discrimination eventually became a major preoccupation with Ambedkar, a lifelong mission. It was in order to fulfil this mission that he turned to religion. His relationship with religion was rather peculiar. He critiqued religion, Hinduism, for giving legitimacy to caste divisions and hierarchy in society. He embraced religion, Buddhism, to overthrow the untouchability and humiliation thrust upon the people of his community in Hinduism. Not only did he work as an intellectual and critic of Hinduism but also as a leader and missionary to mobilize the humiliated people for a dignified existence.

Christophe Jaffrelot (2004; 2009) identifies four different strategies that Ambedkar deployed in his struggle against caste inequalities and untouchability, spanned over the thirty years of his active political career. First of all, he worked towards building a respectable identity for them, to produce an alternative history of them, a history that gives them a sense of dignity and explains their subordination without justifying it. His second strategy was the engagement with 'electoral politics'. The third important strategy that Ambedkar used to uplift his people was to 'work with rulers, from British Raj to the Congress Raj'. Finally, and most importantly, was his decision to convert, along with his people, out of Hinduism.

Though B.R. Ambedkar had visualized the neo-Buddhist movement to be a movement of all the Dalits of the subcontinent, it remained confined mostly to Maharashtra and to the community of Mahars, to which Ambedkar himself belonged. The other states where it found some appeal have been Tamil Nadu (Aloysius 1998) and Uttar Pradesh (Joshi 1977). However, despite its limited influence in terms of conversions to Buddhism, Ambedkar's critique of Hinduism has acquired wider acceptance among Dalit communities of the country (Jaffrelot 2004) and his persona has come to be accepted as a symbol of Dalit identity almost everywhere. It has given them a sense of confidence, a new identity of not being untouchables (Zelliot 1970; 1977).

Another important and effective Dalit movement was the Ad Dharam movement in Punjab (Juergensmeyer 1988). Juergensmeyer argues that the Ad Dharam movement was a direct product of new economic opportunities opened up by the British colonial rule in the region. After conquering the region, the British set up a cantonment in the Jallandhar town of Punjab, which significantly raised the demand of leather goods such as boots and shoes required for the British army. The erstwhile dominant Muslim traders could not fulfil the new demand. Some enterprising members of the local Dalit Chamar community, who were already involved with leather work, took advantage of the emerging situation and joined in the business, which brought some prosperity to some Chamars of the Doaba region of Punjab. The introduction of secular education by the colonial rulers and Hindu reformers also helped these upwardly mobile Dalits in developing a new political outlook.

Mangoo Ram, whose father was one such enterprising Dalit Chamar, had his initial education in a school opened by Hindu reformers, the Arya Samajis. After graduating from school, his father sent Mangoo Ram to California for employment. However, he returned after a few years to work for his community. He initially worked with the Arya Samaj but soon broke off from them and initiated an autonomous movement of the untouchable communities. He argued that untouchables were a *qaum*, a distinct religious community similar to that of Muslims, Hindus, and Sikhs, and that the qaum had existed from times immemorial, even before Hinduism emerged (Juergensmeyer 1988: 45). His strategy was to acquire the status of a religious community outside Hinduism and consequently, outside the system of caste hierarchy. When the 1931 Census approached, the Ad Dharmis insisted they be listed as a separate religious community and not be clubbed with the Hindus. Interestingly, their demand was accepted by the colonial rulers.

A total of 4,18,789 persons reported themselves as Ad Dharmis in the 1931 Punjab Census, almost equal to the Christian populace of the province. They accounted for about 1.5 per cent of the total population of Punjab and around a tenth of the total low-caste population of the province. Nearly 80 per cent of the low castes of Jallandhar and Hoshiarpur districts reported themselves as Ad Dharmis (Ibid.: 77). Though they did not identify with the Sikh religion, they looked towards it for alternative sources of religious and ritual life. Sikhism was easier to engage with, because not only did it theologically oppose caste, the Sikh holy book, Guru Granth, also included the writings of Ravi Das.

However, despite its success, the movement could not maintain its momentum for long and began to dissipate soon after its grand success in 1931. Perhaps the main cause of its decline lay in its success. Its leaders joined mainstream politics. Mangoo Ram himself was elected to the Punjab Legislative Assembly. The introduction of the reservation policy also required that Ad Dharmis identify themselves as Hindus in order to qualify for the Scheduled Caste (SC) status. They eventually began to be treated as a sub-caste of the Chamar Dalits of Punjab. However, the movement did give a sense of dignity and confidence to its members, which also translated into a new energy and aspiration for mobility. Ad Dharmis and Ravi Dasis of Punjab are among the most mobile of the SCs in contemporary India.

From Untouchables to Dalits

The rise of Dalit consciousness and their efforts to break away from the traditional social order was rarely easy or a simple affair. Dalit assertions have, almost everywhere, invoked violence and atrocities against them (Omvedt 1995: 73). Professional sociologists have often observed that though the practice of untouchability began to slowly decline during the post-independence period, atrocities against Dalits have been rising (Béteille 2000; Shah 2000). In the emerging scenario, the Dalit movements also began to change their orientation and focus, from religious conversions to civil rights and seeking citizenship status.

Perhaps the first important movement in this category was the formation of the Dalit Panthers during the early 1970s. It was in 1972 that a group of young Dalits, mostly writers and poets came together in Bombay (Mumbai) under the name of Dalit Panthers. However, this movement was not confined to Maharashtra alone. As atrocities began to be reported from different parts of the country, so did the news of new forms of Dalit organizations and protests. Its larger context has been well articulated by Gail Omvedt in the following words:

> ... it was a period in which atrocities against Dalits in the villages, often of brutal and horrifying forms, seemed on the increase.... Whatever its form in each region, a new movement was enveloping most of the country ... (1995: 73–4)

Unlike the earlier movements that looked at Indian society and its caste system as being culturally unique, Dalit Panthers drew parallels between caste and race and compared themselves with the Blacks. Even the name of their organization suggests that they were inspired by the Black Panther movement of the United States (Joshi 1986). They were perhaps the first ones to articulate the caste question in the language of rights.

This shift was also enabled by the change in the wider context. Thanks to the official policy of quotas or reservations for SCs, a new educated and urban middle class began to emerge from within the Dalit communities. By the early 1980s their absolute numbers had become quite substantial, spread across urban centres of the country. Their articulation of the caste question also reflected their experience of working in urban settings, in government offices along with members of upper castes. Many of them initially tried to assimilate in the mainstream middle-class life. However, they soon realized that it was not very easy to get away from their caste identity.

These middle-class Dalits started forming separate groups and unions of their own. They also formed Dalit cultural groups and study circles. It was from these initiatives that a broader Dalit identity began to be articulated at the national level and new social and political movements of Dalits began to emerge in different parts of the country (Zelliot 2001; Shah 2001; Hardtmann 2009). It is this new brand of Dalit activists which is carrying forward the agenda of Dalit rights. As Hardtmann writes: 'The Dalit movement has grown tremendously all over India since the beginning of 1990s. Today, its networks are spread across the globe, including Dalit activists in the diaspora ...' (2009: xii).

Globalization has a very specific value for Dalit politics and mobilizations. From inward-looking reforms and Sanskritization, Dalit movements have moved to a global stage where they compare themselves with other groups and communities that experience discrimination because of their descent, ethnicity, colour, and race. This has also given them new alliances and platforms for articulating their grievance and winning support/alliances. These wider processes, however, do not mean that there are no ground-level mobilizations of Dalits, or that untouchability or caste atrocities can be fought without engaging with the local-level realities. However, the local is no longer isolated from the global. The processes of globalization and articulation of the Dalit question in global forums, or by the Dalit diaspora in the West and by international development actors, influence and shape local-level articulations of the caste question and Dalit rights. These are important questions that need to be researched. Dalit movements are not movements of the past. They are ongoing and emerging processes.

State Policy and Contesting Caste from Above

Apart from the mobilizations and protests by those at the receiving end of the system, the modern-day political establishment has also introduced policies and legislations that attempt to democratize Indian society and minimize the influence of caste in the public sphere. As discussed earlier, state processes such as enumeration, its bureaucratic theorizations, and its modes of categorizing/classifying the population for administrative purposes played a role in shaping our understanding of caste. These processes also influenced the way caste communities looked at themselves or constructed their identities, which in turn have had a bearing on the way individuals and groups related to each other.

It was during the British colonial rule that the 'untouchable' communities of the subcontinent began to attract state attention for welfare and development. As we have seen in the previous chapter, the British rulers clubbed them together and made them into an administrative category, initially calling them 'depressed classes', and later listing them as SCs in the Government of India Act of 1935. The post-independence Indian state continued with the category of SCs but expanded the list of communities and scope of state action. Over the years the Government of India has evolved a large number of policies and programmes for the welfare and empowerment of SCs.

Broadly speaking, we could identify three sets of policy measures that the Indian State evolved to deal with the marginalized situation of the SCs. These are (i) protective measures in the form of legal sanctions against the practice of untouchability and violation of civil rights; (ii) enabling or empowering measures in the form of special programmes for their development including a system of quotas in state-run educational institutions and in employment in the government system and State-funded organizations; and (iii) representational measures in the form of special quotas in legislative bodies at all levels in proportion to their population.

Protective Measures

Introduction of constitutional democracy granted citizenship rights to all. The Constitution of India unequivocally abolished the practice of untouchability in any form. Article 17 of the Indian Constitution made the practice of untouchability an offence. It stated unambiguously: '"Untouchability" is abolished and its practice in any form is forbidden. The enforcement of any disability arising out of "Untouchability" shall be an offence punishable in accordance with law.'

However, given that Indian society was based on hierarchical values of caste, the exercise of citizenship rights by Dalits often generated social tension leading to attacks on Dalits by the so-called upper castes. In response the Government of India also enacted several legislations to protect Dalits from violence of different kinds. The Untouchability Offence Act was passed in 1955 followed by the Protection of Civil Rights Act in 1976 and the Scheduled Castes and Scheduled Tribes Prevention of Atrocities Act in 1989. Besides these, several provincial/state governments also enacted legislations focusing on 'removal of civil disabilities'. Though most of these legislations were passed during the post-independence period, the process, as discussed earlier, had actually begun in the nineteenth century.

The Government of India also developed administrative structures to oversee the working of various safeguards provided to the Scheduled Caste (SC) and Scheduled Tribe (ST) communities. Article 338 of the Indian Constitution provided for appointment of a Special Officer, designated as Commissioner for SCs and STs, who was assigned the duty to investigate all matters relating to the safeguards for SCs and STs in various statutes and report directly to the President of India about the working of these safeguards. It was to extend and consolidate this function that in 1978 the Government of India decided to set up a multi-member commission, called the National Commission for Scheduled Castes and Scheduled Tribes. In 2004, the Government of India decided to divide this Commission into two separate Commissions dealing respectively with SCs and STs.

Enabling Measures

Apart from making 'untouchability' a legal offence and initiating measures to extend citizenship status to those who had traditionally been on the margins of Indian society, the Government of India also introduced several enabling measures designed to create a level playing field for these historically deprived social groups, the SCs and STs. The first and most important of these measures was the introduction of a quota system—reservations of seats in government-run educational institutions and for employment in government or state-sector jobs.

Second, the central and state governments also introduced various development schemes/programmes

directed at enabling SCs and STs to actively participate in the emerging economy and new avenues of
employment. These included different kinds of schol-
arships for Dalit students as well as special credit and
employment schemes for the self-employed. From the
Sixth Plan onwards, the state governments were also
required to have a separate Plan for the Welfare of SCs,
the Special Component Sub Plan under which they
were required to set aside an amount of their budget
for various welfare activities meant for the SCs. The
quantified amount required for this Plan had to be in
proportion to the SC population in the state. Every
state government also had to have a separate department dealing with the welfare of the SCs and oversee-
ing various schemes for their development.

Some of these programmes have produced discern-
ible results. For example, there has been a significant
increase in levels of literacy and education among the
SCs. As shown in Table 2, the total literacy rate among
SCs went up from a mere 10.27 per cent in 1961
to nearly 55 per cent in 2001, bringing them much
closer to the general population than was the case in
1961. Interestingly, literacy grew at a much faster rate
among them than in the general population. School

attendance also improved bringing them close to the general/other categories of population. For example, in 2001 as many as 72 per cent of the SC boys (Others 77) and 63 per cent of SC girls (Others 70 per cent) in the age group of 6 to 14 were attending schools.

However, not everything is worth celebrating. Apart from gender differences in literacy rates and school attendance, there are also significant variations across regions. For example, in Bihar, where SCs constitute 16 per cent of the total state population, their literacy rate continues to be abysmally low at 28.5 per cent. Also, their numbers decline as we go up the educational ladder.

Perhaps more serious are the growing disparities in the quality of schooling. With economically better-off sections, mostly from the upper-caste categories, withdrawing from the government-run schools the quality of schooling available to the poor has further gone down. Dropout rates for the SC children are also much higher than others. According to the 2004–5 data, more than 34 per cent of SC children dropped out of school by the time they reached Class V while the overall percentage was 29. This gap between the dropout rate of SCs and 'Others' increases as we go up the education ladder (Dasgupta and Thorat 2009: 15). This high dropout rate among SC children is not merely because of economic compulsions. In some instances, caste discrimination is also responsible for the feeling of alienation that Dalit children experience in school. There are instances where separate pots for drinking water are still kept in schools for Dalit children in some parts of India (see Shah et al. 2006).

TABLE 2 Literacy Rate of the General Population and SC Population, 1961–2001

Year	General			SC		
	Male	Female	Total	Male	Female	Total
1961	34.44	12.95	24.02	16.96	3.29	10.27
1971	39.45	18.70	29.45	22.36	6.44	14.67
1981	46.89	24.82	36.23	31.12	10.93	21.38
1991	64.1	39.3	52.2	49.91	23.76	37.41
2001	75.3	53.7	64.8	66.64	41.90	54.69

Source: Calculated from Census of India data, as in *The Eleventh Five Year Plan* (2008), Volume 1. Available at http://planningcommission.nic.in/plans/planrel/fiveyr/11th/11_v1/11th_vol1.pdf (p. 105), accessed on 20 October 2009.

As mentioned earlier, the Government of India also introduced quotas for SCs and STs in the state-sector jobs. Notwithstanding various criticisms of job reservations from within the SC communities and from outside, it has been one of the most successful programmes of affirmative action in the world today. Apart from giving employment to eligible Dalit candidates, the job quotas also helped produce a new leadership, an elite, from within the SC communities. These new community elite in turn are playing a very critical role in articulating their aspirations in the social and political domain.

As per the data available from different sources (see Table 3) we can see that there has been a remarkable increase in the proportion of SC employees at various levels of employment in the state sector. Given their social conditions and the near complete absence of education, they could be hired only at the lowest level. However, even Class IV (Group-D) jobs in the state sector meant a regular and much higher income than what they could earn living in the village. More importantly, a government job invariably also made them move to urban centres where they could send their wards to better schools. Given the assured pensions of a government job, many of them could permanently move to urban living. Their children could use the quota system to gain access to higher education and higher-level jobs. As is evident from Table 3, over the years, their representation has grown at all the levels of government sector employment. In 1965, the proportion of SCs in Group-A jobs was 1.64 per cent and in Group-B jobs was 2.82 per cent. However, over the years, their proportion in the higher category jobs kept increasing and by 2003 it had gone up to 11.93 and 14.32 per cent for categories 'A' and 'B', respectively. Their proportion in Group-C jobs also saw a steady increase over the years.

Empowering Measures

As mentioned earlier, employment in the government sector at the senior level not only gave the individual employee better salaries and a sense of dignity, but it also created a resource for the historically deprived communities, social capital or a new network of contacts in the state departments that provided a channel of mobility to other members of the communities as well. Their presence in senior positions in public institutions become particularly critical in events of crisis, such as caste-related conflicts where Dalits are almost always at the receiving end because of the overall power of dominant castes.

TABLE 3 Percentage Share of SCs and Non-SCs/STs to Total Employees in Government Jobs by Category (Excluding Sweepers)

Year	Group A SC	Group A Non-SC/ST	Group B SC	Group B Non-SC/ST	Group C SC	Group C Non-SC/ST	Group D SC	Group D Non-SC/ST
1965	1.64	97.59	2.82	96.56	8.88	89.71	17.75	78.82
1968	2.11	97.30	3.11	96.48	9.22	90.65	18.32	78.08
1971	2.58	97.01	4.06	95.51	9.59	88.74	18.37	77.98
1972	2.99	96.52	4.13	95.43	9.77	88.52	18.61	77.57
1973	3.14	96.36	4.51	95.00	10.05	87.99	18.37	77.70
1974	3.25	96.18	4.59	94.92	10.33	87.54	18.53	77.64
1975	3.43	95.95	4.98	94.43	10.71	87.02	18.64	77.37
1981	5.46	93.42	8.42	90.28	12.95	83.90	19.35	75.57
1982	5.49	93.34	9.02	89.55	13.39	83.14	23.41	69.14
1984	6.92	91.38	10.36	87.87	13.98	82.23	20.20	73.77
1985	7.65	90.62	10.04	88.39	14.88	80.92	20.81	73.49
1987	8.23	89.72	10.41	87.67	14.45	81.32	20.04	74.12
1988	8.67	89.04	11.18	86.72	14.80	80.72	19.88	74.02
1989	8.51	89.25	11.65	86.35	14.85	80.63	20.41	73.13
1990	8.64	88.78	11.29	86.32	15.19	79.98	21.48	71.79

1991	9.09	88.37	11.82	85.83	15.65	79.36	21.24	71.94
1992	9.67	87.40	11.57	86.05	15.74	81.10	20.88	72.37
1993	9.80	87.13	12.17	85.48	15.91	78.66	20.73	72.39
1994	10.25	86.83	12.06	85.13	15.73	78.88	20.47	73.38
1995	10.15	86.96	12.67	84.65	16.15	78.16	20.53	72.99
1996	11.51	84.93	12.30	84.89	15.45	78.90	20.27	73.67
1997	10.74	86.03	12.90	84.05	16.20	77.65	24.06	69.21
1998	10.80	85.76	12.35	84.63	16.32	77.67	18.65	74.40
1999	11.29	85.32	12.68	83.98	15.78	78.15	19.99	73.00
2000	10.97	85.55	12.54	84.37	15.88	77.79	17.38	75.95
2001	11.42	85.00	12.82	83.48	16.25	77.29	17.89	75.30
2002	11.09	84.94	14.08	81.74	16.12	77.94	20.07	72.80
2003	11.93	83.88	14.32	81.36	16.29	77.17	17.98	75.06

Source: Thorat and Senapati (2006: 18).

Besides these policies of positive discrimination in government jobs, the Indian Constitution also made provisions for reservation of seats for SCs and STs in legislative bodies and other representational institutions as per their proportions in the total population. From panchayats to the Parliament, Dalit presence in the elected bodies has become ubiquitous. At a sociological level, these measures have also played an important role in producing a new political class among the Dalits and they are now present in all political parties. Given that on a constituency-reserved post for SCs, only an SC candidate can contest, it has become imperative for all political parties to cultivate a constituency among the SCs and provide space to them in the organizational establishment of their parties. The SC candidates also act as pressure lobbies within political parties on questions concerning their communities.

More recently we have seen the rise of identity-based political parties in different parts of India. These political parties openly identify themselves either with a specific caste community, or they claim to represent a cluster of caste communities, such as Dalits and/or 'Backward Castes'. While most of them are region-based political parties, some of them have also emerged or aspire to emerge as national parties. The rise and success of the Bahujan Samaj Party in north India is a good example of this.

Besides the changes that the movements against caste hierarchy and the State action have been able to infuse in the traditional hierarchy, the caste system has also been changing due to the broader processes of social and economic transformation that the Indian society has been experiencing over the last century. The following chapter attempts an overview of these changes.

5

Caste Today

As any other aspect of social life, the institution of caste is dynamic. However, the nature and pattern of change varies with time. Notwithstanding its origin in the ancient past, the idea of caste, as we know it today through academic writings and popular imagination, began to be shaped only during the British colonial period. Our detailed discussion in the first chapter clearly shows that in its modern format caste was conceptualized in the nineteenth century by the colonial administrators, as a type of traditional system of social organization, comparable to similar institutions found in the pre-modern periods of other societies. In the Indian case, caste acquired a rigid form because of its association with Hindu religion. Thus, notwithstanding its local specificities, the system of caste hierarchy was placed by the colonial and orientalist scholarship in a universal evolutionary schema. An obvious corollary of this argument was that as the traditional belief systems and forms of social organization declined, caste would also lose its hold and eventually disappear. In other words, we had to simply grow out of caste, in a kind of linear progression, and this was to happen with the natural process of growth and material progress, almost inevitably.

This perspective on caste also underlined the point that caste was primarily a cultural or ideological system, a traditional way of life, and had little or nothing to do with material/economic life, or with the power and politics of the day. As an ideological system and an aspect of Hindu religion, caste was about ritual status and social hierarchy. According to this understanding of caste, in the past when regimes of power changed, the ritual order of hierarchy survived. Thus, unlike the inequalities of class, which had to be fought over and struggled with, this 'mainstream' discourse on caste provided very little space for human agency. Caste appeared like a 'natural' system of hierarchy, which was to disappear 'naturally', with the process of evolution and modernization.

The popular middle-class and academic view on the modern Indian history has tended to look at the colonial period as a progressive phase, particularly in relation to institutions like caste. For example, it is widely perceived that the British colonial rule brought about a paradigm shift in Indian society because they introduced modern technology and the Western value system in the subcontinent, which, presumably, were superior and more advanced than what prevailed in India at that time.

The Modernity of Caste

As discussed in the previous chapters, the underlying assumption of this formulation of the caste system and its evolution has many flaws.

The changes introduced by the British colonial rulers in the social and economic life of India were indeed very drastic. They introduced a completely new set of land revenue systems and forms of property relations, which over the years, began to transform the rural social relations quite drastically. They also brought new technology to India. They laid railway lines and opened factories that ran on inanimate sources of energy. They also introduced the Western style 'secular' education system. They opened schools and colleges to educate Indians in the English medium. The first 'modern' universities in the subcontinent were also opened during the colonial period. Though a large majority of those who were enrolled in the English medium schools, colleges, and universities came from the traditionally privileged classes and upper castes, in principle, these institutions were open to all, irrespective of caste, creed, and colour. A new social category, the Indian middle class began to emerge under the colonial patronage. Admittedly, there was a considerable overlap 'between the traditional and new elite' and it often resulted in increasing 'cultural and ideological distance between the high and the low castes' (Srinivas 1968: 193).

The British colonial rulers also evolved a new administrative and legal system. In order to make administration effective, they initiated the process of enumeration of the subject population through censuses and surveys. Enumeration required classification and categorization of the population. Though the ideas of pollution and hierarchy had existed almost everywhere in the subcontinent, the order and arrangements of those hierarchies were local or regional. As concrete social institutions, each caste group had a local universe within which it operated and reproduced itself. The order of hierarchy was also reproduced in relation to the material universe of agrarian economy, prevailing power regimes and social demographics. For example, different caste groups have had different relationships with land. While some owned and cultivated land, some were not even allowed to touch the plough by the prevailing customs. Each region had its own set of dominant and influential caste groups. Agrarian economy and village economy had been integrated into the State system much before the British came to India (Habib 1963; Neal 1962). As Manor rightly points out 'India has not one caste system but many' (2010: xx). Similarly, Gupta (2000) has also argued that models of hierarchies were multiple, and often contested. Though hierarchy had a religious sanction, its reproduction also depended on the prevailing economic relations of structures of power and domination.

The processes of enumeration and classification introduced by the colonial rulers generated a new dynamics of social aggregation and differentiation. As discussed in Chapter 3, the clubbing of several castes into the category of depressed classes based on the official acceptance of the idea of 'pollution-line', which eventually translated into the category of 'Scheduled Castes', produced a bipolar model of caste division— 'touchables' and 'untouchables'. It was not only in relation to the Scheduled Castes (SCs) that the colonial state played a defining role. The colonial Census made the state-system a critical agent in the life of all castes. The process of enumeration had brought in the idea of 'numbers' as a crucial variable in the local imaginations of caste communities. Thus, along with the ritual status, the numerical strength of a group also began to acquire significance, particularly when it came to the question of recognition and representation in the evolving state system.

As we have discussed in detail, by the early decades of the twentieth century, different caste groups had begun to organize themselves in the form of 'caste associations', a process that had been completely unknown until then. With the formation of associational identities a new sense of competitiveness also developed among different caste groups. Though they all deployed the idiom of caste, something new was happening to caste.

It began to be articulated and mobilized on horizontal lines, as regional-level pressure groups. They raised the questions of representation and equity. The so-called backward castes of the Madras Presidency were perhaps the first to organize themselves against the 'upper'-caste Brahmins. They demanded quotas for the 'backwards' in government jobs, which, as mentioned above, had been a virtual monopoly of the Brahmins and other upper castes. As discussed in Chapter 4, though the anti-Brahmin movement did not raise the question of untouchability, their criticism of the caste system paved the way for the rise of Dalit movements in Maharashtra and elsewhere in the following decades.

Caste, Communities, and Development

As it would appear from the available literature on caste in modern India and the discussion above, by the time India gained independence from the colonial rule, organizationally and ideologically, the order of caste had been dented. Abolition of the practice of untouchability and expansion of the quota system by the Indian Constitution further reinforced the point that modern India did not uphold the normative order of caste. The State policy of affirmative action, the reservations, was designed to create a level playing field, where each caste group could compete on equal footing.

The change, however, had its limitations. The anti-caste movements had mostly been urban-centric, with focus on the concerns of the upwardly mobile Backwards and Dalits. A large majority of the ex-untouchables, however, lived in rural areas and were employed either in the traditional callings of their castes or as agricultural labourers. While the welfare and developmental programmes provided them new sets of opportunities, only a minuscule proportion of them could avail of such benefits. More important, perhaps, even though the Indian Constitution provided reservations for the SCs and also abolished the practice of untouchability, the mainstream process of development planning was largely 'caste-blind'. The development machinery worked with categories like rich and poor, or peasants, farmers, and labourers. During the initial decades, caste was rarely treated as a relevant variable in the visualization, designing, or administration of various developmental schemes and programmes. However, the process of development did have implications for the prevailing structure of caste relations.

For example, one of the most important developmental initiatives taken by the Indian State soon after independence was the introduction of Land Reform legislations. These legislations were designed to weaken the hold of the non-cultivating intermediaries (the so-called landlords) by transferring ownership rights to the tillers of the land. Even though Land Reform legislations were only partially successful, they played an important role in weakening the hold of the traditionally powerful but numerically small groups of upper castes over the rural social order (Moore 1966; Frankel and Rao 1989; Jaffrelot 2000; Stern 2001). In a village in Rajasthan, for example, though the 'abolition of *jagirs*' (intermediary rights) was far from satisfactory, it made considerable difference to the overall land ownership patterns, and to the local and the regional power structures. The Rajputs, traditionally upper caste and the erstwhile landlords, possessed far less land after the Land Reforms than they had done before. Most of the village land moved into the hands of those who were traditionally identified as tillers of the land, the middle caste groups such as Jats and Gujars.

However, only rarely did these land reforms benefit the Dalits. Though a large majority of local Dalits also laboured on land, they were not seen as 'tillers of the land', and hence not entitled to receive land under the Land Reforms. Similarly, other initiatives for rural social change, such as the Community Development Programme (CDP), Panchayati Raj, and the Green Revolution, directly helped the rich and powerful in the village, further consolidating the position of the locally dominant castes, often to the detriment of ex-untouchable communities.

The rise of regional political parties during the 1960s and 1970s in different parts of India was a direct consequence of the growing power of these rural/ agriculture-based dominant castes. This rise of middle-level castes during the 1960s also brought about a change in the landscape of democratic politics in the country. While in some regions the Congress Party was able to accommodate the growing aspirations of these middle-level caste groups, it could not do so everywhere (Jaffrelot 2003). It was in this context that regional politics began to acquire increasing significance. The general election of 1967 is believed to have been the turning point in Indian politics. For the first time during the post-independence period, the Congress Party was defeated in as many as eight states. From then on, the flavour of regional politics changed significantly. While in some cases these agrarian castes formed their own political parties, elsewhere they emerged as powerful factions within the national party, the Indian National Congress, invariably around a caste identity. Over the years, they were able to virtually oust the ritually pure upper castes from the arena of state/regional politics.

However, by the 1980s India began to witness new trends in the domain of caste politics. The introduction of separate quotas for the Other Backward Classes (OBCs) by the then Prime Minister, V.P. Singh, on the recommendations of the Mandal Commission in 1990 revived the question of group-based representations, and gave a new political space to caste, normalizing it as 'a mode of doing politics'. However, this resurgence of caste in its new avatar, as Srinivas famously put it (Srinivas 1996) was not merely a consequence of the act of wily politicians who, one fine morning, decided to implement the Mandal Commission Report on reservations for 'Other Backward Classes' in an attempt to consolidate their votes. It was also not simply a case of tradition reasserting itself due to the oft-quoted weaknesses of Indian modernity. Caste appeared in a very different mode during the 1990s. In fact, some important processes that began to unfold themselves around this time expanded the meanings of caste-based politics in democratic India.

The Rise of Dalit Politics

Notwithstanding their participation in competitive politics, and the growing 'secularization' of the public sphere, castes groups remain unequal. Inequalities of caste were never confined to the ritual domain alone. They were far more pervasive. In most of mainland India, the differences of caste-shaped economic structures and conditioned opportunities. While the domain of democratic politics is open to all, different social groups enter democratic politics with different kinds of resources. For example, it was rather easy for the middle-level landowning dominant castes to enter the domain of democratic politics and politicize their caste communities into powerful 'vote-banks' within a decade of the introduction of democratic politics. On the other hand, those at the bottom of the caste hierarchy continued to experience social and political exclusion.

Caste

In fact, in some regions, the rise of middle-level caste groups in state politics meant a stronger master to deal with for the Dalits at the village/local level.

The growing consolidation of democratic politics at the grassroots brought about some important changes in the grammar of Indian politics. Political scientists described this as a shift from the 'politics of ideology' to the 'politics of representation' (Yadav 1999; Palshikar 2004). This shift was clearly evident during the 1980s and 1990s and was visible in the nature of social and political mobilizations that appeared during this period, the so-called 'new social movements'. Besides mobilizing masses from the margins, these movements criticized the prevailing popular wisdom on questions of developmental and social change, being pursued with much enthusiasm by the Indian state. Interestingly, this was also the time when the Indian state itself initiated a process of economic reforms. The following decade saw the beginning of liberalization policies and a gradual withdrawal of the State from the economic sphere and an end of the Nehruvian framework of development.

This shift also prompted the rise of identity politics of different kinds. In this new context the question of caste also began to be articulated in the language of identity politics by Dalit groups in different parts of the country (see Jodhka 2001). Though, as discussed in Chapter 4, Dalit politics had emerged during the colonial period under the leadership of people like Jyotiba Phule and B.R. Ambedkar, until the 1980s, the Dalit question mostly remained subsumed within the nationalist agenda for development. Electorally, the SC communities were mostly aligned with the 'main-stream' political formation, the Congress Party. The autonomous identity politics of the Dalits was con-fined to only a few pockets, in states like Maharashtra, Karnataka, or Andhra Pradesh, and was largely a concern of urbanized individuals who articulated the question of Dalit identity through literature and other cultural forms (Mendelsohn and Vicziany 2000).

However, over the years the size of the Dalit middle class grew, thanks largely to the policy of reservations in government jobs and educational institutions. As they grew in numbers, they also felt more confident in articulating their experiences of discrimination at the workplace, and the continued caste-based prejudice against their communities in the society at large. They began to form separate associations of SC employees, and mobilized themselves during events of discrimination suffered by their caste fellows. It was around this time that Ambedkar was 'rediscovered' as a universal icon of Dalit identity and a symbol of their aspirations (Zelliot 2001).

These new developments in the larger ideological and social environment were happening at a time when rural India was experiencing disintegration in its traditional social and power arrangements. The ritually 'pure' dominant castes who had gained from the institutionalization of democratic politics and rural development programmes initiated by the Government of India during the first three decades of independence also began to experience internal differentiation. Those in the upper segments of the rural economy began to look towards cities for further mobility (Jodhka 2006) and those at the bottom began to question their continued subordination. The experience of participation in the democratic political process over three to four decades also gave those at the bottom a sense of confidence and self-worth.

However, as mentioned earlier, until the 1980s, there was very little evidence to suggest that the democratic politics and development programmes were leading to democratization of rural India. In caste terms, rural power revolved around the landowning dominant caste, and in class terms, it was the rich land-owners and moneylenders who continued to control the rural economy (Thorner 1956). Independent studies by scholars from different regions tended to suggest that the village panchayats continued to function as an arena of power and patronage with the tradition-ally dominant groups at the centre stage (Frankel and Rao 1990).

However, more recent studies tend to suggest a loosening of the traditional structures of power/domination and disintegration of rural hierarchies. On the basis of his fieldwork, Oliver Mendelsohn, for example, argued that by the late 1980s, the idea of dominance of the 'dominant caste' no longer made sense in rural Rajasthan. The 'low caste and even untouchable villagers were now less beholden to their economic and ritual superiors than was suggested in older accounts' (Mendelsohn 1993: 808). Similarly, 'land and authority had been de-linked in village India and this amounted to an historic, if non-revolutionary transformation' (Ibid.: 807).

Writing on the basis of his field experience in Karnataka, Karanth (1996) argued that the traditional association of caste with occupation was weakening, and that jajmani ties were fast disintegrating. In an extensive survey of fifty-one villages of Punjab, I too found a similar change taking place in rural Punjab, where the older structure of jajmani or *balutedari* relations had nearly completely disintegrated (Jodhka 2002b). Except for a few occupations, the old association between caste and occupation could no longer be seen in rural Punjab. Further, Dalits in Punjab had also begun distancing themselves from the village economy, and disliked working on farms owned by the local Jats. They were also trying to construct their own cultural centres like religious shrines and community halls in order to establish their autonomy in the rural power structure.

In the emerging scenario, local Dalits had begun to assert for equal rights and a share from the resources that belonged commonly to the village, and had so far been under the exclusive control of the locally dominant caste groups or individual households. This new-found sense of entitlement and assertion among Dalit communities was directly responsible for the frequent caste-related conflicts and violence being reported from rural Punjab (Jodhka and Louis 2003). A study from rural Bihar also reported a similar erosion of traditional jajmani ties. Here too, the village community's hold over the individuals' choice of occupation was virtually absent (Sahay 2004).

It is in this changed context of a combination of factors that one has to locate the new agency among the Dalits. The new class of political entrepreneurs that has emerged from amongst the ex-untouchable communities used the idea of 'Dalit identity' and mobilized the SC communities as a united block on the promise of development with dignity. Some of them, such as Kansi Ram and Mayawati, have been quite successful in doing so (Shah 2001; Pai 2002).

Almost everywhere Dalits have become much more assertive about their human and political rights (Mendelsohn and Vicziany 2000:1). Whatever might have been the situation in the past, today very few among the ex-untouchables would accept their low status as a naturally given reality or accept it simply as their fate (Charsley and Karanth 1998). Today they 'all aspire to more comfortable material circumstances; all demand more dignity' (Deliège 1999:1).

Caste Matters

This, however, does not necessarily mean that their social conditions have become more comfortable or liberating. Some scholars have, in fact, argued that while ideologically caste has considerably weakened and older forms of untouchability are receding, atrocities committed on Dalits by the local dominant castes have increased, at least in some parts of the country (Béteille 2000; Shah 2000; Mohanty 2007). After an exhaustive review of cases of atrocities against Dalits, a senior political scientist concludes, 'The cumulative picture that emerged from this body of data suggests that the intensity of violence against the dalits has increased even though in some years there may have been a decline in the number of reported atrocities' (Mohanty 2007: 4).

The rise of the Dalit identity and their growing participation in democratic politics is indeed an evidence of a positive change and weakening of the power of caste. However, as mentioned earlier, different caste groups participate in economic and political life with different sets of resources. While it has become quite difficult for locally dominant groups to prohibit the traditionally marginalized caste communities from participating in the political process, this has not meant an end of social inequalities or caste and rank. Being a Dalit, or in some cases OBC, continues to be a marker of disadvantage and social exclusion. The fact that caste violence is almost always a one-way process where Dalits end up at the receiving end also says enough about the continued inequalities of caste groups.

Affirmative action and other state policies have indeed had a positive impact on the Dalits of India. Similarly, legislative measures have also made a difference and have become useful tools in the hands of civil rights organizations and Dalit activists in their struggle for development and empowerment. However, given the rigidity of caste relations and hold of the traditional mindset, the Dalit situation has not seen a radical change. Even where capitalist relations have become dominant in the economic sphere, caste has not necessarily given way to class-like identities. Caste prejudice and caste-based social exclusion continues to be a fact of urban life in contemporary India as well. Empirically, studies show that 'returns to education are often lower among Dalits than others' (World Bank 2011b).

TABLE 4 Percentage of Landless and Near-landless Households according to Land Possessed by SC Households, 1999–2000

State	Landless	Near-landless	Landless Plus Near-landless
Andhra Pradesh	6.9	64.70	71.60
Assam	2.5	56.10	58.60
Bihar	23.8	67.10	90.90
Gujarat	18.1	61.20	79.30
Haryana	5.7	86.10	91.80
Himachal Pradesh	0.9	68.40	69.30
Jammu and Kashmir	0.5	51.90	52.40
Karnataka	3.6	59.30	62.90
Kerala	4.2	89.60	93.80
Madhya Pradesh	13.7	33.9	47.60
Maharashtra	16.7	54.80	71.50
Orissa	1.4	67.1	68.50
Punjab	12.2	82.50	94.70
Rajasthan	3	37.30	40.30
Tamil Nadu	15.1	73.60	88.70
Uttar Pradesh	5.3	66.50	71.80
West Bengal	6	76.20	82.20
India	10	65.00	75.00

Source: Thorat (2009: 251).

The same appears to be the case with their economic position. Comparatively speaking, a larger proportion of SCs live in poverty and deprivation than the non-Scheduled Castes. This is particularly so with those living in rural India. A greater proportion of Dalits live in rural areas than other categories of Indian population and are employed in insecure informal sector jobs. As is evident from Table 4, nearly 75 per cent of Dalits in India are either landless or near-landless. In the states of Bihar, Haryana, Punjab, and Kerala the proportion of such households is above 90 per cent. The obvious implication of such a scenario is that they can find employment only in low-paying labouring jobs. In the year 1999–2000 among the total rural SC households, there were as many as 61.42 per cent labouring households. In contrast, a much smaller proportion (32 per cent) among the non-SC/ST rural households was employed in labouring jobs (as in Thorat 2009: 253).

Caste in the Urban Labour Markets

The disintegration of the village social order has indeed been an empowering change for those at the bottom of the caste hierarchy. A larger number of them now look around for employment outside the village and agrarian economy. Availability of employment in agriculture has also declined over the years. This is particularly so in the prosperous agrarian pockets where the second phase of mechanization has significantly reduced demand for manual labour. However, being asset-less and poor, it is not very easy for them to find viable employment out of the village and the agrarian economy. Those who move to the city invariably end up in informal sector jobs where wage rates are low and insecurities high. For example, against a mere 8 per cent from the so-called general category, as many as 29 per cent of the SCs were part of the casual labour force in 2004–5 (see Table 5). Their proportion in the self-employed category is also significantly lesser, which is a reflection of low employment-generating asset ownership among them. Though in urban areas the SCs are likely to find regular employment in the government sector, here too they are invariably over-represented at the lower end. For example, more than 65 per cent of the sweepers in the Central government ministries are Dalits, invariably from caste communities that were traditionally engaged with the scavenging occupation. In contrast, only '2 per cent of Scheduled Caste prime age working individuals are in higher paying professions or technical occupations compared to 8 per cent of general caste households' (World Bank 2011a: 231).

TABLE 5 Type of Employment across Different Caste
Categories

Employment type	SC	OBC	General	All
Self-employment	28	41	37	38
Regular employment	9	9	14	10
Casual labour	29	16	8	17
Not in labour force	30	32	38	33

Source: World Bank (2011a: 231), based on 2004–5 NSSO Data.

Notwithstanding the promise of inclusive development, the process of globalization and liberalization has not always worked in favour of Dalits. One of the immediate effects of the new economic policy has been the steady decline in the availability of jobs in the state sector where Dalits have the chance of securing a job under the quota system.

Interestingly enough, it is at the middle and lower levels, where Dalit presence has generally been on the higher side that jobs have shrunk. As is evident from Table 6, while the overall share of Dalits in government jobs has remained more or less stable at around 17 per cent between 1994 and 2004, the number of jobs where Dalits were employed went down from 6,02,670 to 5,21,423. Further, while the number of SCs in government jobs went up in Group A and B catego-

TABLE 6 SC Representation in Central Government Services in 1994, 1999, and 2004

Group	1994			1999			2004		
	Total	SCs	% of total	Total	SCs	% of total	Total	SCs	% of total
A	59,016	6,046	10.25	93,520	10,558	11.29	80,011	9,744	12.2
B	1,03,198	12,442	12.06	1,04,963	13,306	12.68	1,35,409	19,602	14.5
C	23,81,613	3,74,758	15.73	23,96,426	3,78,115	15.78	20,40,970	3,44,865	16.9
D	10,23,285	2,09,423	20.47	9,49,353	1,89,761	19.99	8,02,116	1,47,212	18.4
Total	35,67,112	6,02,670	16.9	35,44,262	5,91,740	16.7	30,58,506	5,21,423	17.05

Source: Annual Reports, DOP&T, Government of India, as in the *Eleventh Five Year Plan*, Volume 1, Planning Commission. Available at http://planningcommission.nic.in/plans/planrel/fiveyr/11th/11_v1/11th_vol1.pdf (p. 107), accessed on 20 October 2009.

ries both in relative and absolute terms, their numbers declined significantly in Group C and D jobs.

Does caste matter in private sector employment? Ownership of private industry in India and elsewhere in the world has historically been concentrated in the hands of a few social/cultural groups and the top jobs were always kept within the family. Recruitments to other jobs were opened to outsiders only when the required personnel were not available within the community or the wider kin-group. Over the last two or three decades there has been a considerable change in the culture of the Indian corporate sector. The big companies are no longer run by members of the family. Even when some members of the family are involved, much of the work is done by professionals who are recruited mostly by 'merit'. While merit has become sacrosanct for the corporate self-image, the hiring process is rarely open. The most popular modes of hiring are through: (i) hiring agencies, the 'head-hunters', (ii) campus interviews, and (iii) internal recommendations. A good amount of work is also done through outsourcing to specialized agencies.

Who is a suitable candidate and how do they judge the merit of those who are selected for the upper-end jobs in the private sector? During a study of corporate hiring managers carried out during 2006 and 2007 in Delhi, Jodhka and Newman (2007) found that the suitability of a candidate is rarely judged on the basis of his or her formal qualification alone. Almost every respondent hiring manager interviewed agreed that one of the most important questions they ask the prospective candidates during the interviews is about their 'family background'. Family background, for them, was important to see the suitability of the candidate to the culture of the company. An equally important factor for hiring at the senior level is the linguistic skill of the candidate, his ability to speak and communicate in English fluently. In other words, the critical qualification was the nature of 'cultural capital' (Bourdieu 1986) one possessed, which even according to the hiring managers was largely a deter- minant of one's caste and place of residence (rural/ urban), which in turn determined the kind of schools one went to.

Another study of the university students in Delhi and their perceptions and experiences of finding a job also found that it was only the students from ex-untouchable communities who were made to carry the burden of their caste background even when they were well-educated and looking for jobs in the urban sector. The prospective employers would invariably ask the students with the SC tag about their views on the caste system and relevance of the reservation policy. Those from the upper castes were never asked such questions. 'When private sector employers raise pointed questions about the legitimacy of reservations, students are placed on the defensive'. The candidates hated being asked such questions. They felt as if 'they were being asked to defend their own biographies' (Deshpande 2011: 182–212).

Apart from cultural capital, the nature of social networks or social capital (Putman 1993) that a person has also determines his or her prospects in the urban market. Caste and family are two critical elements of social capital in India and they impact prospects of economic mobility differently for different caste groups. For example, the prospects of those coming from lower down in the caste hierarchy trying to set up independent business in urban centres are often conditioned by their caste situation. First of all, historically those from the ex-untouchable communities not only owned little agricultural land they also had no access to credit and capital. However, over the last two decades, some of them have ventured into the urban economy and have tried to start their own businesses. What has been their experience?

In a recent survey of Dalit entrepreneurs in the urban centres of Haryana and Uttar Pradesh (Jodhka 2010), it was found that they almost always lacked economic resources when compared with their counterparts from other communities. Even when they had economic resources they were crippled by a lack of social resources. This was particularly true about certain caste groups among the Dalits. While Chamars, who have traditionally been involved with some kind of businesses and have been producers and providers of leather, were relatively more successful in running urban businesses, Balmikis seemed to be much more disadvantaged, socially and economically.

In the traditional urban centres of India, business works through cartels and they are mostly formed on caste and kinship lines. This is particularly true about the small-scale businesses/industries in small towns. These cartels are invariably controlled by the traditionally dominant business caste groups in the region. As has been shown by studies from elsewhere, community and kinship networks have always played a very crucial role in businesses (Rutten 2003; Munshi 2007). For those coming from the ex-untouchable communities, deficits of cultural and social capital are not the only problems. They also encounter strong 'collective prejudice' originating from tradition, which not only cripples their prospects in the market but also shapes their self-image and the levels of confidence. In other words, they almost always experience caste as discrimination.

Postscript

This 'short' introduction has attempted to present the different dimensions of caste in an accessible language but without compromising on the complexities of the subject. My attempt has been to provide a broad overview of the various perspectives and diverse experiences of caste, as they have been discussed and written about by social scientists. As I have tried to show, the meaning and experience of caste changes, depending upon whose experience of caste is given priority.

The classical Dumontian perspective on the subject, as various scholars have shown, presented caste as it appeared in the classical Hindu texts, written mostly by the Brahmins, and thus presented a story of caste that the Brahmins would want to tell. Caste, in this view, was an institution that had its origin in Hindu religion. Its core feature was its ideological character. In this perspective, the ideology of caste shaped social interaction among the Hindus, their life-worlds and identities, personal and social. Caste, according to this view, was a distinctive feature of Indian civilization, not to be found anywhere else in the world. Though the notions of hierarchy and inequality were the core features of 'caste', it was, above all, a cultural reality. It was fundamentally different from the concept or category of 'class', a feature of the Western societies where inequalities originated from the realities of economic and political life. As an Indian or Hindu tradition, caste was a system of status hierarchies that worked independently of the material world of power and economic relations.

As we have discussed in different chapters of the book, very few scholars today agree with such a view of caste.

While the system of status hierarchy is central to caste and it indeed has an ideological dimension, its reproduction could not happen independently of the political and economic processes. The Hindu mind is no unique thing. More importantly perhaps,

171

differences of caste do not exist only among the Hindus of the South Asian region. They exist among other religious communities as well, albeit in diverse ways. The empirical studies of caste by scholars using different perspectives show that caste was closely tied to power and economy. For example, the system of caste hierarchy directly shaped agrarian or land relations, which in turn, played a critical role in its reproduction. As historians have shown through their research on medieval and ancient India, caste and custom determined who could 'plough' and/or 'own' land and who could not. Given that caste and land relations were intrinsically tied, they fashioned economic inequalities and were closely tied with the political regimes of the times. Historical research has shown that our knowledge about caste has been shaped also by statecraft, the manner in which the British colonial rulers classified the native population into different categories.

As discussed in Chapter 2, empirical studies of the Indian village carried out by social anthropologists during the 1950s and 1960s clearly showed that caste was a dimension of power. These studies also showed that the ground realities of caste varied from region to region. Invariably, Brahmins enjoyed high status only in regions where they were big landowners and had been close to the regimes of power. There was no dissonance between power and status. In some regions of the subcontinent, such as the Punjab, Brahmins were considered dispensable. But the institution of caste remained strong. Thus the perspective on caste that emerges from historical and empirical studies presents a different picture of caste hierarchy.

Another popular myth about caste has been its unchanging and uncontested nature. This too has been contradicted amply by the historical and empirical literature. As I have discussed in Chapters 3 and 4, those located at the bottom of the caste hierarchy often question its legitimacy. Even when they accepted the framework of hierarchy, the individual communities contested their position in the system of hierarchy, sometimes through the popular 'origin myths' of their caste communities, and sometimes through collective mobilizations. For those located below the 'line of pollution', caste has always been a source of 'humiliation' that reinforced their subordinate status in society and produced violence, deprivations, and hunger.

The pace of change in caste relations was indeed accelerated during the post-independence period, by the state policies of affirmative action and by the structural changes in the Indian economy, the processes of 'modernization' and development. The shift from a traditional agrarian and rural society to a modern industrial economy has implications for every aspect of human social life. Not only do these processes of social and economic transformation change the context and content of relations among the various castes on the ground, but it also alters the internal structure of caste communities. Irrespective of their location, caste communities have been experiencing a process of internal differentiation. Some become poor, some rich and some remain in-between. It is becoming increasingly difficult to associate a particular caste group with a specific occupation or a specific way of life.

Where do we go from here? How should we talk about caste, if we must?

Some would argue that in the contemporary context, beyond kinship-related affairs, caste has become largely insignificant. This is particularly so in urban India. Though differences and inequalities may continue to exist in public life, or may even have become sharper, their character has changed. Today they are shaped by the capitalist economy and, thus, they

174

are primarily economic in nature and ought to be seen in terms of class differences, a common feature of all modern societies. Even if there is an occasional or frequent overlap of a modern occupation and caste, it should be seen as an incidental fact, not determined or conditioned by past traditions of caste hierarchy.

Some others would reinforce this argument by saying that caste persists in present-day India primarily because of its uses in democratic politics, or because of the caste-based quotas. Had it not been for the political entrepreneurs who mobilize caste communities as 'vote banks', it would have virtually disappeared by now. Participation of caste-based communities in competitive politics also implies that they have effectively become equal and the traditional hierarchical system of occupational and social segregation has lost all its ideological moorings. Caste groups have transformed themselves into ethnic communities and traditional hierarchies have been reduced to mere cultural or notional differences. They survive as ethnic identities because it serves the interest of the newly emergent elite within these caste communities.

While these arguments have indeed become popular with the urban middle classes, they are not entirely sustainable. As we have seen in Chapters 4 and 5, for a large majority of those located below the 'line-of-pollution', the ex-untouchables or SCs and those located immediately above this line, the so-called lower-OBCs, the legacy of caste continues to be a major source of deprivation. As the official data shows, the proportion of poor and landless/assetless is significantly higher among them, when compared to those from the so-called general category. Though the reach of formal education has expanded over the last fifty years or so, the quality of education available to them is far from satisfactory. Their children do get enrolled in schools, but a large proportion of them tend to drop out before completing ten years of schooling. The reason for their dropping out is directly linked to their caste situation. Even those who manage to get to colleges or professional degree courses continue to experience prejudice in the labour markets. The legacy of caste is hard to erase for those coming from the lower end of the 'traditional hierarchy'. Caste, for many of them, continues to matter beyond kinship and family values. It is a source of deprivation, denial, and discrimination.

The contemporary discourse of caste is thus, not about tradition or village social life. It is framed in the context of the widely accepted normative parameters of inclusive citizenship, universal entitlements, participatory democracy, and the challenges of institutionalizing them.

References

Aggarwal P.C. 1983. *Halfway to Equality*. New Delhi: Manohar Publications.

Aloysius, G. 1998. *Religion as Emancipatory Identity: Buddhist Movement among the Tamils under Colonialism*. New Delhi: New Age International Publishers.

Ambedkar B.R. 1937/2007. *Annihilation of Caste*. New Delhi: Critical Quest.

———. 2002. 'Caste in India', in Ghanshyam Shah (ed.), *Caste and Democratic Politics in India*, pp. 83–107. Delhi: Permanent Black.

Appadurai, Arjun. 1988. 'Putting Hierarchy in Its Place', *Cultural Anthropology,* 3(1): S.36–49.

Arnold, David, Robin Jeffrey, and James Manor. 1976. 'Caste Associations in South India: A Comparative Analysis', *Indian Economic and Social History Review*, 23(3): 353–73.

Bailey, F.G. 1960. *Tribe, Caste and Nation*. Bombay: Oxford University Press.

Bailey, F.G. 1963. 'Closed Social Stratification in India', *European Journal of Sociology,* 4(1): 107–24.

Beltz, J. 2005. *Mahar, Buddhist and Dalit.* New Delhi: Manohar.

Berreman, Gerald D. 1963. *Hindus of Himalayas: Ethnography and Change.* Berkeley: University of California Press.

———. 1991. 'The Brahamanical View of Caste', in Dipankar Gupta (ed.), *Social Stratification,* pp. 87–8. New Delhi: Oxford University Press. (First published in *Contributions to Indian Sociology* (n.s.), 5(1): 16–25).

Béteille, André. 1970. 'Caste and Political Group Formation in Tamilnad', in Rajni Kothari (ed.), *Caste in Indian Politics.* Hyderabad: Orient Longman.

———. 1971/1996. *Caste Class and Power: Changing Patterns of Stratification in Tanjore Village.* New Delhi: Oxford University Press.

———. 1986. 'Individualism and Equality', *Current Anthropology,* 27(2): 121–34.

———. 2000. 'The Scheduled Castes: An Inter-regional Perspective', *Journal of Indian School of Political Economy,* 12(3–4): 367–80.

Bouglé, C. 1958. 'The Essence and Reality of Caste System', *Contributions to Indian Sociology,* II(1): 7–30.

———. 1971. *Essays on the Caste System.* Cambridge: Cambridge University Press.

Bourdieu, Pierre. 1986. 'The Forms of Capital', in John G. Richardson (ed.), *Handbook of Theory and Research for the*

Sociology of Education, pp. 241–58. New York: Greenwood Press.

Burghart, R. 1978. 'Hierarchical Models of the Hindu Social System', *Man*, New Series, 13(4): 519–36.

Charsley, Simon R. 1996. '"Untouchable": What is in a Name?', *Journal of the Royal Anthropological Institute* (n.s.) 2(1): 1–23.

Charsley, S.R. and G.K. Karnath. 1998. *Challenging Untouchability: Dalit Initiative and Experience from Karnataka*. New Delhi: Sage Publications.

Cohn, B.S. 1968. 'Notes on the History of the Study of Indian Society and Culture', in Milton Singer and B.S. Cohn (eds), *Structure and Change in Indian Society*, pp. 3–28. New York: Aldine Publishing Co.

———. 1987. *An Anthropologist among Historians and Other Essays.* Delhi: Oxford University Press.

———. 1996. *Colonialism and Its Forms of Knowledge: The British in India*. Princeton: Princeton University Press.

D'Souza, Victor S. 1967. 'Caste and Class: A Reinterpretation', *Journal of Asian and African Studies*, 2(1): 192–211.

Das, Veena and J.P.S. Uberoi. 1971. 'The Elementary Structures of Caste', *Contributions to Indian Sociology* (n.s.), 5: 33–43.

Dasgupta, B. (ed.) 1978. *Village Studies in the Third World*. Delhi: Hindustan.

Dasgupta P.D. and S.K. Thorat. 2009. 'Will India's Attainment of MDGs be an Inclusive Process?', *IIDS Working Paper Series*, 3(2), Indian Institute of Dalit Studies, New Delhi.

Deliège, Robert. 1993. 'The Myth of Origin of the Indian Untouchables', *Man*, New Series, 28(3): 53–49.

―――. 1999. *The Untouchables of India*. New York: Berg Publishers.

Deshpande, Ashwini. 2011. *The Grammar of Caste: Economic Discrimination in Contemporary India*. New Delhi: Oxford University Press.

Deshpande, S. 2003. *Contemporary India: A Sociological View*. New Delhi: Penguin.

Dirks, N. 1989. 'The Original Caste: Power, History and Hierarchy in South Asia', *Contributions to Indian Sociology*, 23(1): 59–77.

―――. 2001. *Castes of Mind: Colonialism and the Making of Modern India*. Princeton: Princeton University Press.

Djurfeldt, G. and S. Lindberg. 1975. *Behind Poverty: The Social Formation of a Tamil Village*. London: Curzon Press.

Dua, V. 1970. 'Social Organization of the Arya Samaj: A Study of Two Local Arya Centres in Jullundur', *Sociological Bulletin*, 19(1): 32–50.

Dube, S.C. 1955. *Indian Village*. London: Routledge and Kegan Paul.

―――. 1955/1960. 'A Deccan Village', in M.N. Srinivas (ed.), *India's Village*. London: Asia Publishing House.

Dumont, L. 1998. *Homo Hierarchicus: The Caste System and Its Implications*. Delhi: Oxford India Paperbacks (first published in 1970).

Frankel, F. and M.S.A. Rao (eds). 1989. *Dominance and State Power in Modern India: Decline of a Social Order*. Delhi: Oxford University Press (Volume I).

—————. 1990. *Dominance and State Power in Modern India: Decline of a Social Order*. Delhi: Oxford University Press (Volume II).

Fuller, C.J. 1977. 'British India or Traditional India? An Anthropological Problem', *Ethnos,* 3(4): 95–121.

—————. 1984. *Servants of the Goddess: The Priests of a South Indian Village*. Cambridge: Cambridge University Press.

Galanter, Marc. 1984. *Competing Equalities: Law and the Backward Classes in India*. Delhi: Oxford University Press.

Gerth, H. and C. Wright Mills. 1948. *From Max Weber: Essays in Sociology*. London: Routledge and Kegan Paul.

Ghuman, Paul. 2011. *British Untouchables: A Study of Dalit Identity and Education*. Burlington: Ashgate.

Ghurye, G.S. 1932. *Caste and Race in India*. London: Kegan Paul.

Gooptu, Nandini. 2001. *The Politics of the Urban Poor in Early Twentieth Century*. Cambridge: Cambridge University Press.

Gorringe, Hugo. 2005. *Untouchable Citizens*. New Delhi: Sage Publications.

Gupta, Dipankar. 1981. 'Caste Infrastructure and Super-structure', *Economic and Political Weekly,* 16 December: 2093–104.

————. 1984. 'Continuous Hierarchies and Discrete Castes', *Economic and Political Weekly*, XIX(46): 1955–8.

————. 2000. *Interrogating Caste: Understanding Hierarchy and Difference in Indian Society.* Delhi: Penguin Books.

Habib, I. 1963. *Agrarian Systems of Mughal India.* Bombay: Asia Publishers.

Hardgrave, R.L. 1969. *The Nadars of Tamilnad: The Political Culture of a Community in Change.* Berkley: University of California Press.

Hardtmann, Eva-Maria. 2009. *The Dalit Movements in India: Local Practices, Global Connections.* Delhi: Oxford University Press.

Hiebert, P.G. 1971. *Konduru: Structure and Integration in a South Indian Village.* Minneapolis: University of Minnesota Press.

Hutton, J.H. 1946. *Caste in India.* Cambridge: Cambridge University Press.

Inden, Ronald. 1990. *Imagining India.* Oxford: Blackwell.

Inkeles, A. and D.H. Smith. 1974. *Becoming Modern— Individual Change in Six Developing Countries.* Cambridge: Harvard University Press.

Irschick, Eugene. 1969. *Politics and Social Conflict in South India: The Non-Brahmin Movement and Tamil Separation 1916–29.* Berkley: University of California Press.

Jaffrelot, C. 2000. 'The Rise of the Other Backward Classes in the Hindi Belt', *The Journal of Asian Studies*, 59(1): 86–108.

————. 2003. *India's Silent Revolution: The Rise of Low Castes in North Indian Politics*. Delhi: Permanent Black.

————. 2004. *Dr. Ambedkar and Untouchability: Analyzing and Fighting Caste*. Delhi: Orient Longman.

————. 2009. 'Dr. Ambedkar's Strategies against Untouchability and the Caste System, *IIDS Working Paper*, 3(4), Indian Institute of Dalit Studies, New Delhi.

Jayal, Niraja Gopal (ed.). 2001. *Democracy in India*. New Delhi: Oxford University Press.

Jodhka, S.S. (ed.). 2001. *Community and Identities: Contemporary Discourses on Culture and Politics in India*. New Delhi: Sage Publications.

————. 2002a. 'Caste and Untouchability in Rural Punjab', *Economic and Political Weekly*, 37(19): 1813–23.

————. 2002b. 'Nation and Village: Images of Rural India in Gandhi, Nehru and Ambedkar', *Economic and Political Weekly*, 37(32): 3343–54.

————. 2006. 'Beyond "Crises": Rethinking Contemporary Punjab Agriculture', *Economic and Political Weekly*, XLI(16): 1530–7.

————. 2009. 'The Ravi Dasis of Punjab: Global Contours of Caste and Religious Strife', *Economic and Political Weekly*, XLIV(24): 79–85.

Jodhka, S.S. 2010. 'Dalits in Business: Self-employed Scheduled Castes in North-west India', *Economic and Political Weekly,* 45(11): 41–8.

Jodhka S.S. and Prakash Louis. 2003.'Caste Tensions in Punjab:Talhan and Beyond', *Economic and Political Weekly*, XXXVIII(28): 2923–6.

Jodhka, S.S. and Katherine Newman. 2007.'In the Name of Globalisation: Meritocracy, Productivity and the Hidden Language of Caste', *Economic and Political Weekly*, 42(41): 4125–32.

Joshi, Barbara R. 1977. 'The Buddhist Movement of Western Uttar Pradesh', Mimeo.

————. 1982.'Whose Law,Whose Order:"Untouchables", Social Violence, and the State in India', *Asian Survey*, 22(7): 676–87.

————. 1986. *Untouchable! Voices of the Dalit Liberation Movement.* London: Zed Books.

Juergensmeyer, M. 1988. *Religious Rebels in the Punjab: The Social Vision of Untouchables.* Delhi: Ajanta Publications.

Karanth, G.K. 1996. 'Caste in Contemporary Rural India', in M.N. Srinivas (ed.), *Caste: Its Twentieth Century Avatar*, pp. 87–109. New Delhi: Penguin.

Khare, R.S. (ed.). 2006 *Caste, Hierarchy and Individualism: Indian Critiques of Louis Dumont's Contributions.* New Delhi: Oxford University Press.

Kothari, Rajni. 1970. *Caste in Indian Politics*. Hyderabad: Orient Longman.

Krishna, Anirudh. 2001. 'What is Happening to Caste? A View from Some North Indian Villages', Terry Sanford Institute of Public Policy Working Paper SAN01-04, Duke.

Lele, Jayant (ed.). 1981. *Tradition and Modernity in Bhakti Movements*. Leiden: EJ Brill.

Lorenzen, David N. 1987. 'Tradition of Non-caste Hinduism: Kabir Panth', *Contributions to Indian Sociology*, 21(2): 263–83.

Lynch, O. 1969. *The Politics of Untouchability: Social Mobility and Social Change in a City of India*. New York: Columbia University Press.

Majumdar, D.N. 1958. *Caste and Communication in an Indian Village*. Bombay: Asia Publishing House.

Manor, James. 2010. 'Prologue: Caste and Politics in Recent Times', in Rajni Kothari (ed.), *Caste in Indian Politics* (Second Edition), pp. xi–lxi. Hyderabad: Orient Blackswan.

Marx, Karl. 1853. 'The British Rule in India', *The New York Herald Tribune*, 10 June 1853. Available at http://www.marxists.org/archive/marx/works/1853/06/25.htm, accessed on 21 December 2011.

Mencher, J.P. 1974. 'The Caste System Upside Down or the Not-So-Mysterious East', *Current Anthropology*, 15(4): 469–93.

Mendelsohn, O. 1993. 'The Transformation of Authority in Rural India', *Modern Asian Studies*, 15(4): 805–42.

Mendelsohn, O. and M. Vicziany. 2000. *The Untouchables: Subordination, Poverty and the State in Modern India*. Cambridge: Cambridge University Press.

Moffat, M. 1979. *An Untouchable Community in South India*. Princeton: Princeton University Press.

Mohanty, M. 2007. 'Kilvenmani, Karamchedu to Khairlanji: Why Atrocities on Dalits Persist?' Available at www.Boell-India.Org/Download_En/Mohanty_Amrita_Corrected. Pdf, accessed on 9 November 2009.

Moore, B. Jr. 1966. *Social Origins of Dictatorship and Democracy: Lord and Peasant in the Making of the Modern World*. Middlesex: Penguin Books.

Munshi, Kaivan. 2007. 'The Birth of a Business Community: Tracing Occupational Migration in a Developing Economy'. Available at www.econ.brown.edu/fac/Kaivan_Munshi/diamond10.pdf, accessed on 10 November 2008.

Neale, W. 1962. *Economic Change in Rural India: Land Tenure and Reform in Uttar Pradesh, 1800–1955*. New Haven: Yale University Press.

Nehru, Jawaharlal. 1946/1992. *The Discovery of India*. Delhi: Oxford University Press.

Omvedt, Gail. 1976. *Cultural Revolt in a Colonial Society: The Non-Brahmin Movement in Western India—1873 to 1930*. Bombay: Scientific Socialist Education Trust.

Omvedt, Gail. 1994. *Dalits and the Democratic Revolution: Dr. Ambedkar and the Dalit Movement in Colonial India.* New Delhi: Sage Publications.

—————. 1995. *Dalit Visions: The Anti-caste Movement and the Construction of an Indian Identity.* New Hyderabad: Orient Longman Ltd.

Omvedt, Gail. 2008. *Seeking Begumpura: The Social Vision of Anti-caste Intellectuals.* New Delhi: Navayana.

Pai, Sudha. 2002. *Dalit Assertion and the Unfinished Democratic Revolution: The Bahujan Samaj Party in Uttar Pradesh.* New Delhi: Sage Publications.

Palshikar, Suhas. 2004. 'Revisiting State Level Politics', *Economic and Political Weekly*, XXXIX(14–15): 1477–80.

Pandian, M.S.S. 1996. 'Towards National-Popular: Notes on Self-Respecters Tamil', *Economic and Political Weekly*, 31(51): 3323–9.

Pimpley P.N. and S.K. Sharma. 1985. '"De-Sanskritization" of Untouchables: Arya Samaj Movement in Punjab', in P.N. Pimpley and S.K. Sharma (eds), *Struggle for Status*, pp. 86–101. Delhi: B.R. Publishing Corporation.

Planning Commission. 2008. *Eleventh Five Year Plan*, Volume 1. Available at http://planningcommission.nic.in/plans/planrel/fiveyr/11th/11_v1/11th_vol1.pdf, accessed on 20 October 2009.

Putnam, Robert D. 1993. *Making Democracy Work: Civic Traditions in Modern Italy.* Princeton: Princeton University Press.

Quigley, D. 1993. *The Interpretations of Caste*. Delhi: Oxford University Press.

Raheja, Gloria G. 1989. 'Centrality, Mutuality and Hierarchy: Shifting Aspects of Inter-caste Relationships in North India', *Contributions to Indian Sociology* (n.s.), 23(1): 79–101.

Rao, M.S.A. 1979. *Social Movements and Social Transformation: A Study of Two Backward Class Movements in India*. New Delhi, Macmillan Press.

Rudolph, Lloyd I. and Susanne H. Rudolph. 1967/1999. *The Modernity of Tradition: Political Development in India*. Hyderabad: Orient Longman Limited.

Rutten, Mario. 2003. *Rural Capitalists in Asia: A Comparative Analysis on India, Indonesia, and Malaysia*. London: Routledge.

Saberwal S. 1976. *Mobile Men: Limits to Social Change in Urban India*. New Delhi: Vikas Publishing House.

Sahay, Gaurang R. 2004. 'Hierarchy, Difference and the Caste System: A Study of Rural Bihar', *Contributions to Indian Sociology* (n.s.), 23(1&2): 113–36.

Shah, Ghanshyam. 1975. *Caste Associations and Political Process in Gujarat: A Study of Gujarat Kshatriya Sabha*. Bombay: Popular Prakashan.

———. 2000. 'Hope and Despair: A Study of Untouchability and Atrocities in Gujarat', *Journal of Indian School of Political Economy*, XII(3–4): 459–72.

———. 2001. 'Dalit Movements and Search for Identity', in G. Shah (ed.), *Dalit Identity and Politics*. New Delhi: Sage Publications.

References

Shah, Ghanshyam (ed.). 2002. *Caste and Democratic Politics in India*. Delhi: Permanent Black.

————. 2004. *Social Movements in India: A Review of the Literature*. New Delhi: Sage Publications.

Shah, Ghanshyam, Harsh Mander, Sukhadeo Thorat, Satish Deshpande, and Amita Baviskar. 2006. *Untouchability in Rural India*. New Delhi: Sage Publications.

Sharma, Satish Kumar. 1985. *Social Movements and Social Change: Study of Arya Samaj and Untouchables in Punjab*. Delhi: B.R. Publications.

————. (ed.). 1987. *Reform Protest and Social Transformation*. New Delhi: Ashish Publishing House.

Sharma, Ursula. 2002. *Caste*. New Delhi: Viva Books Private Limited.

Srinivas, M.N. (ed.) (1955) *India's Villages*. London: Asia Publishing House.

————. 1959. 'The Dominant Caste in Rampura', *American Anthropologist*, 61: 1–16.

————. 1962. *Caste in Modern India and Other Essays*. Bombay: Media Promoter and Publishers.

————. 1966. *Social Change in Modern India*. Berkley: University of California Press.

————. 1968. 'Mobility in the Caste System', in Milton Singer and Bernard S. Cohn (eds), *Structure and Change in Indian Society*. New York: Aldine.

————. 1972. *Social Change in Modern India*. Berkeley: University of California Press.

Srinivas, M.N. 1976. *The Remembered Village*. Delhi: Oxford University Press.

———— (ed.). 1996. *Caste: Its Twentieth-century Avatar*. New Delhi:Viking.

Stern, R.W. 2001. *Democracy and Dictatorship in South Asia: Dominant Classes and Political Outcomes in India, Pakistan, and Bangladesh*. Cambridge: Cambridge University Press.

Tandon, Praksh (1961) *Punjabi Century 1857–1947*. New York: Harcourt, Brace and World.

Thapar, Romila. 1975. *The Past and Prejudice*. New Delhi: National Book Trust.

Throat, Sukhadeo. 2009. *Dalits in India: Search for a Common Destiny*. New Delhi: Sage Publications.

Thorat, Sukhadeo and Chittaranjan Senapati. 2006. 'Reservation Policy in India—Dimensions and Issues', *IIDS Working Paper Series*, I(2), Indian Institute of Dalit Studies, New Delhi.

Thorner, D. 1956. *The Agrarian Prospects in India*. Delhi: University Press.

Wilkinson, T.S. and M.M. Thomas (eds). 1972. *Ambedkar and the Neo-Buddhist Movement*. Madras: Christian Literary Society.

Wiser, W.H. 1936/1969. *The Hindu Jajmani System*. Lucknow: Lucknow Publishing House.

World Bank. 2011a. *Perspectives on Poverty in India: Stylized Facts from Survey Data*. Washington DC: The World Bank.

World Bank. 2011b. *Poverty and Social Exclusion in India*. Washington DC: The World Bank.

Yadav, Y. 1999. 'Electoral Politics in the Time of Change: India's Third Electoral System, 1989–99', *Economic and Political Weekly*, 34(34–5): 2393–9.

Zelliot, E. 1970. 'Learning the Use of Political Means: The Mahars of Maharashtra', in R. Kothari (ed.), *Caste in Indian Politics*. New Delhi: Orient Longman.

———. 1977. 'The Psychological Dimension of the Buddhist Movement in India', in G.A. Oddie (ed.), *Religion in South Asia: Religious Conversions and Revival Movements in South Asia in Medieval and Modern Times*. London: Curzon Press.

———. 2001. *From Untouchable to Dalit: Essays on the Ambedkar Movement*. New Delhi: Manohar (Third Edition).

Index